Python Passive
Network Mapping

Python Passive Network Mapping

P2NMAP

Chet Hosmer

Technical Editor
Gary C. Kessler

AMSTERDAM • BOSTON • HEIDELBERG • LONDON
NEW YORK • OXFORD • PARIS • SAN DIEGO
SAN FRANCISCO • SINGAPORE • SYDNEY • TOKYO
Syngress Publishers is an Imprint of Elsevier

Acquiring Editor: Chris Katsaropoulos
Editorial Project Manager: Benjamin Rearick
Project Manager: Priya Kumaraguruparan
Designer: Matthew Limbert

Syngress is an imprint of Elsevier
225 Wyman Street, Waltham, MA 02451, USA

British Library Cataloguing-in-Publication Data
A catalogue record for this book is available from the British Library

Library of Congress Cataloging-in-Publication Data
A catalog record for this book is available from the Library of Congress

ISBN: 978-0-12-802721-9

For information on all Syngress publications
visit our website at http://store.elsevier.com/

Working together
to grow libraries in
developing countries

www.elsevier.com • www.bookaid.org

To our children who inspire me every day and make me realize how blessed I truly am. Whether you take care of the sick and injured, you teach and inspire future generations, you care deeply and fight to protect our environment or you simply bring unconditional love to everyone you touch. To Kira, Tiffany, Trisha and Matty.

Contents

Biography

Chet Hosmer is the Founder of Python Forensics, Inc. a non-profit organization focused on the collaborative development of open-source investigative technologies using the Python programming language. Chet is also the founder of WetStone Technologies, Inc. and has been researching and developing technology and training surrounding forensics, digital investigation and steganography for over two decades. He has made numerous appearances to discuss emerging cyber threats including National Public Radio's Kojo Nnamdi show, ABC's Primetime Thursday, NHK Japan, CrimeCrime TechTV and ABC News Australia. He has also been a frequent contributor to technical and news stories relating to cyber security and forensics and has been interviewed and quoted by IEEE, The New York Times, The Washington Post, Government Computer News, Salon.com and Wired Magazine.

Chet serves as a visiting professor at Utica College where he teaches in the Cybersecurity Graduate program. He is also an Adjunct Faculty member at Champlain College in the Masters of Science in Digital Forensic Science Program. Chet delivers keynote and plenary talks on various cyber security related topics around the world each year.

Chet resides with Wife Janet, Son Matthew along with his four legged family near Myrtle Beach, South Carolina.

Gary C. Kessler, Ph.D., CCE, CCFP, CISSP, is a Professor of Homeland Security at Embry-Riddle Aeronautical University, a member of the North Florida ICAC (Volusia County Sheriff's Department), and president and janitor of Gary Kessler Associates, a training and consulting company specializing in computer and network security and digital forensics. He is the co-author of two professional texts and over 70 articles, a frequent speaker at regional, national, and international conferences, and past editor-in-chief of the Journal of Digital Forensics, Security and Law. More information about Gary can be found at his Web site, http://www.garykessler.net.

Preface

It is Monday morning, July 6, 2015 and you have just returned from the long holiday weekend. On your desk sits a note that reads…

> A vulnerability has been discovered that may affect SCADA based networks. We need to determine if any of our systems are potentially vulnerable or worse have already been compromised. As you know, we <u>cannot</u> actively scan our SCADA network, so we need to passively map network activity and behaviors over the next week and then analyze the results. We need a way to determine/verify every end point on our network, what systems they communicate with, what countries those connections have made to and from. I Need prelim report by noon tomorrow.
>
> Thanks,
>
> the CISO
> P.S. we have no budget for new toys.

INTENDED AUDIENCE

This information in this book was designed to be accessible by anyone who has a desire to learn how to leverage the Python programming language to passively monitor and analyze network activity for <u>worthy causes</u>. The open source scripts and knowledge transfer are yours to use and hopefully inspire you to advance the scripts, contribute to the community, and look at passive network monitoring from a whole new perspective.

PREREQUISITES

Access to a computer, familiarity with an operating system (Windows, Linux or Mac) and access to the Internet, coupled with a desire to learn. Some familiarity with programming and the Python programming language would be helpful.

READING THIS BOOK

The book is organized with the first two chapters focused on introductory material to define what passive network mapping is, how to setup an environment to perform passive network mapping, and to demonstrate what value passive network mapping can bring.

Chapters 3 and 4 introduce scripts that perform passive network capture on a Linux or Windows platform, and provides scripts that allow you to perform network mapping functions and mine the captured data for analysis purposes.

Chapter 5, provides a script that can convert existing packet capture files (.pcap) into the structure necessary to perform network mapping, analysis and OS Fingerprinting. In addition, Chapter 5 develops a model and working script that performs OS Fingerprinting using only passively observed data.

Chapter 6 then presents future predictions, observations along with a series of challenge problems for future work.

SUPPORTED PLATFORMS

All the examples in the book are written in Python 2.7.x in order to provide the greatest platform compatibility.

The P2NMAP-Capture.py script has been validated on Linux and Windows operating systems.

The P2NMAP-Analyze.py script, P2NMAP-PCAP-Extractor.py script and P2NMAP-OS-Fingerprint.py scripts have been validated for Linux, Windows and Mac.

DOWNLOAD SOFTWARE

Those purchasing the book, will also have access to the open source code examples in the book for easy use, enhancement and continued research. The scripts and text have been created for easy integration into graduate and undergraduate classrooms, training courses and hands on lab environments.

The source code is available from the python-forensics.org web site.

COMMENTS, QUESTIONS AND CONTRIBUTIONS

I encourage you to contribute in a positive way to this initiative. Your questions, comments and contributions to the source code library and enhanced passive OS

Fingerprint dataset will benefit the whole community. www.python-forensics.org will make these resources available to all.

Finally, I challenge you all to share your ideas, knowledge and experience.

Sincerely,

Chet Hosmer

Acknowledgments

My sincerest thanks go to:

Dr. Gary Kessler, the technical editor for this book. Gary is everything you could want from a technical editor … not only does he find all my technical errors, but he also brings great ideas to the table. Thank you Gary, your constant encouragement and friendship made the process fun.

Chris Katsaropoulos, Ben Rearick, Steve Elliot, and the whole team at Elsevier for your enthusiasm for this topic, and all the guidance, patience and support along the way.

To Janet, for helping to make every chapter better, more consistent and always finding just the right quote to kick off each chapter.

And to the whole team at WetStone … Carlton, Tiffany, Geoff, Amanda, Heather, Brian and Sean for making it possible for me to begin the next chapter of my career.

## CHAPTER 1

Introduction

"Measure what is measurable, and make measurable what is not so."

Galileo Galilei

CONVENTIONS USED IN THIS TEXT

I use standard typographical conventions (bold, italics, etc.), to highlight text that stands out from the overall body of the paragraph. The font styles I will be using throughout the text are:

Italic
  Used for file and directory names and to emphasize terms
`Constant width`
  Used for code listings and script generated output
`Constant Width and `**`Bold`**
  Used for user input

Enterprise Networks today are complex, difficult to investigate, require specialized tools and demand exceptional and expert skills in order to properly respond to incidents. When dealing with incidents that involve critical infrastructure or other regulated industry environments the specialization of the toolkits can indeed be daunting.

One of the first challenges that face incident response teams and forensic investigation units is "What does your network consist of and how is it configured?" This may seem like a simple question that is easily answered by the Information Technology group. However, when responding to incidents like *Heartbleed*, *Operation Shady Rat*, and breaches at major retailers, the technical information and details regarding the network map can be vital.

More specific questions may also include:

- What internet protocol (IP) addresses and subnets do you operate?
- What servers and end points are running?
- Are the Servers local, hosted at an external site or in the cloud?

FIGURE 1-1 Enterprise Networks.

- What Operating Systems are in use? What versions and are they up-to-date?
- What Services (open ports) are available on each server and host?
- What applications and databases are in use?
- How is your network configured, protected and isolated?
- What connections are allowed between servers, hosts and Internet users?
- What connections have occurred recently?
- Are the activities from or to specific end points anomalous?
- Where are those connections (*to* and *from*)? If the connection include hosts outside the internal network where are these connections physically located in the world? Can they be pinpointed and verified?

If some or all of these questions can be answered the follow-up questions are of course:

- How do you know? ...and
- Are you sure?

Typically these answers come from the Chief Information Officer (CIO) or the directed IT personnel responsible for the network along with the (Chief Information Security Officer) CISO and related cyber security staff members. Each of these groups utilize a variety of tools to assist in managing the cyber assets under their control. These tools can range from a simple set of spreadsheets to complex asset control inventory and management systems, or in the worst case, stored between the ears of the staff members themselves. Don't get me wrong, many of these folks are very talented and have a pulse and deep understanding of the networks they manage. All of this information regardless of its source or form factor is important and valuable to incident response and forensic investigation teams. They of course have the arduous task of determining what is happening or has happened, who is doing it, how to mitigate and remediate the damage and better defend against future incidents. All of the data regardless of the means of collection however, is necessary to execute a comprehensive forensic investigation.

Python Passive Network Mapping: P²NMAP - An open source solution to uncovering nefarious network activity deals with the challenge "what does your network consist of and what are identifiable or unusual behaviors?" Traditionally, network mapping is an *active process* whereby IT and cyber teams utilize tools to identify network based assets.

Nmap, (Network Mapper - a security scanner originally written by Gordon Lyon - also known by his pseudonym Fyodor Vaskovich) used to discover hosts and services on a computer network, works by communicating raw IP packets to specified IP address ranges to determine:

- what hosts exist within the range
- what services are running on each of the discovered hosts
- what operating system are those host likely to be running

…and a plethora of other characteristics that can be tested and measured through this active interrogation method.

By way of a quick introduction let's take a look at the current instantiation of Nmap for Windows using the Zenmap Graphical User Interface (GUI).

Figure 1-2 depicts the main display of Nmap running under the Zenmap GUI version 6.47. Zenmap is a multi-platform graphical front-end that interfaces

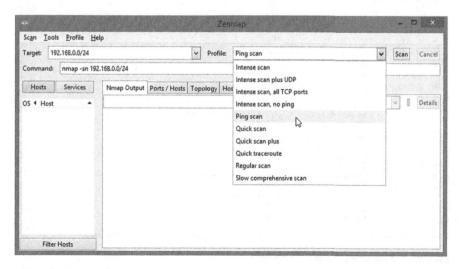

FIGURE 1-2 Nmap Today.

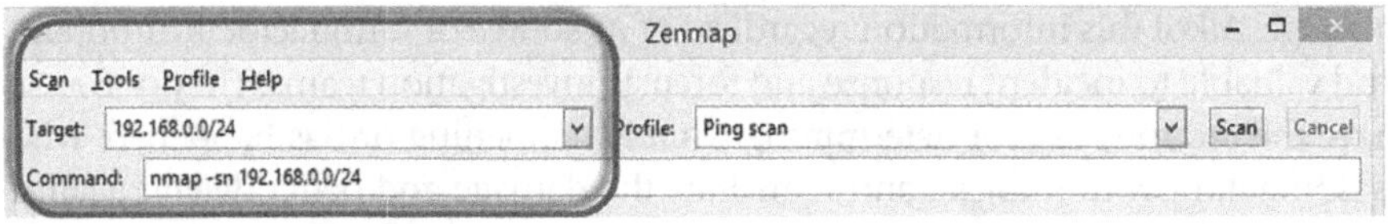

FIGURE 1-2A Ping Scan Selection.

with the standard command line of Nmap and then displays the results in a more useable and interactive format.

As you can see in Figure 1-2A, I have selected a simple ping Scan with a target selection of 192.168.0.0/24. Zenmap displays the exact Nmap command that will be executed based on the selections that I have made. Dissecting the command reveals the specific instructions delivered to the Nmap engine.

```
nmap -sn 192.168.0.0/24
  |    |       |__ IP Address and range
  |    |___ specifies a simple ping scan only
  |___Nmap command
```

The results of this quick scan can be seen in Figure 1-3. As you scan through the list of computers and other devices on my local network you might find some interesting hits and responses.

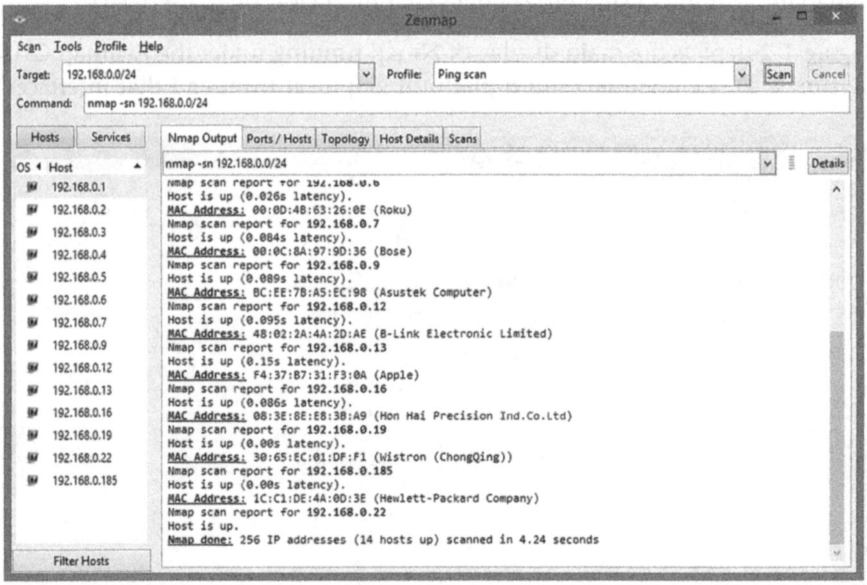

FIGURE 1-3 Summary Results of Ping Scan.

1. IP address 192.168.0.7 was identified as a Roku box used for streaming content from the Internet.
2. IP address 192.168.0.7 was identified as our Bose Wave Radio.
3. IP address 192.168.0.13 was identified as our B-Link surveillance camera, just in case you had thoughts about stealing the Bose wave radio. :)
4. IP address 192.168.0.16 identified as an Apple device, ….this could be one of many
5. IP address 192.168.0.19 is a DirecTV receiver
6. IP address 192.168.0.185 is an Internet radio
   Along with several other typical computers. (My wife was a computer scientist also… thus the 'several'!) It is important to note, that the manufacturer identification of these devices is not based on any Nmap magic, but rather on the OUI (Organizationally Unique Identifier) portion of the MAC address.
   This provides a pretty good scan of the active devices on my local network. Of course these are the devices that responded to scan. What about the printers and other mobile devices that were not identified? We will be discussing this issue throughout the book.

If you are a more visual person, Figure 1-4 provides a graphical view of the network IP addresses identified. This allows users to drill down into specific devices and discover additional information.

So What is a Ping Anyway?

Ping is the cyber equivalent of traditional SONAR (short for SOund Navigation And Ranging), or the "pings" that are used to locate objects under water. A cyber ping actually refers to the use of a special network protocol namely the *Internet Control Message Protocol (ICMP)*. It is primarily used by network devices to send error messages indicating that specific services are unavailable or unreachable, or to communicate and query specific status.

For host discovery purposes, ICMP's *Echo Request* message is used to make a request to a specific IP addresses and then wait for the associated *Echo Reply Type Message*. Traditional thinking is that if you cannot obtain a response from a host that you ping, other services offered are likely unavailable. In many cases when troubleshooting connection issues ping is used to verify connectivity to a specific IP address.

> Due to increased concern and awareness of cyber security issues many network firewalls and gateways block *ICMP Echo Requests* to stop unauthorized mapping of hosts on the network. Unfortunately, this plays both ways as insiders that wish to add hosts to the corporate network will configure their systems to block *ICMP Echo Requests* as well and therefore will not be discoverable using this type of scan.

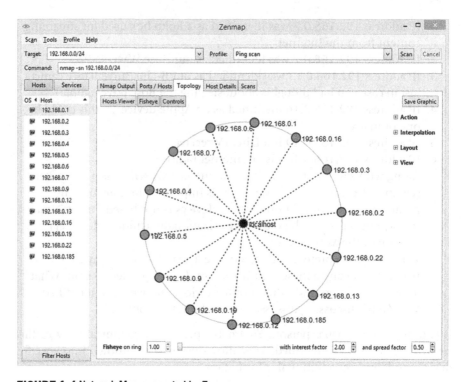

FIGURE 1-4 Network Map generated by Zenmap.

ICMP is part of the Internet Protocol Layer as shown in Figure 1-5 and ICMP messages are transmitted using IP datagrams as depicted in Figure 1-6.

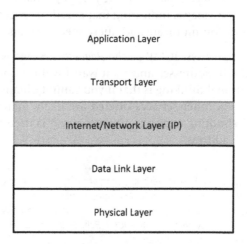

FIGURE 1-5 Example Internet Protocol Stack Layers.

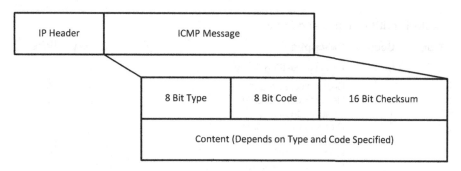

FIGURE 1-6 ICMP Message Contained Within and IP Datagram.

Many message types and codes exist as shown in Table 1-1 on the following page. For our use in host discovery, the highlighted *Echo Request Type 8, Code 0* and *Echo Reply Type 0, Code 0* represent our primary use. However, as you can see, ICMP has many other Types and Codes that are used by network devices. Note ICMP is an IP Type 1 message.

To provide a quick demonstration, I configured a simple network made up of just 4 computers as shown in Figure 1-7.

In this example, using the ping command, I sent *ICMP* Request Type Packets from 192.168.0.5 → 192.168.0.9. IP address 192.168.0.9 responded with the appropriate response message.

```
chet@PythonForensics:~$ ping 192.168.0.9
PING 192.168.0.9 (192.168.0.9) 56(84) bytes of data.
64 bytes from 192.168.0.9: icmp_req=1 ttl=64 time=279 ms
64 bytes from 192.168.0.9: icmp_req=2 ttl=64 time=201 ms
64 bytes from 192.168.0.9: icmp_req=3 ttl=64 time=122 ms
64 bytes from 192.168.0.9: icmp_req=4 ttl=64 time=40.6 ms
64 bytes from 192.168.0.9: icmp_req=5 ttl=64 time=269 ms
64 bytes from 192.168.0.9: icmp_req=6 ttl=64 time=197 ms
```

You might notice that the packet delays are timed and range from 40.6 ms to 279 ms. This may seem unusual to you. I chose this specific target IP address, (as shown in Figure 1-3, this is my Bose Wave Radio), to show the response to pings. As you can see responses from this device are a bit erratic in comparison to a typical desktop computer. Also, you may notice that each of the ICMP requests contain a different sequence number denoted as icmp req = 1, icmp req = 2, ... icmp req = 6. This is because the ping command employs a monotonically increasing value starting at 1, since IP packets, by their definition, are unreliable (or, better defined, as best effort), and packets can be lost, respond out of sequence, or be delayed. Finally, you notice that the ping request includes

Table 1-1 ICMP Types and Codes

Type	Code	Description	Query	Error
0	0	Echo Reply (Ping Reply)	☑	
3		Destination Unreachable		☑
	0	Network Unreachable		☑
	1	Host Unreachable		☑
	2	Protocol Unreachable		☑
	3	Port Unreachable		☑
	4	Fragmentation Error		☑
	5	Source Route Failure		☑
	6	Destination Route Failure or Unknown		☑
	7	Destination Host Unknown		☑
	8	Obsolete		☑
	9	Destination Network Blocked		☑
	10	Destination Host Blocked		☑
	11	Network Unreachable		☑
	12	Host Unreachable		☑
	13	Communication Filtered		☑
	14	Host Precedence Violation		☑
	15	Precedence Cutoff		☑
4	0	Source Quench		☑
5		Redirect		☑
	0	Network Redirect		☑
	1	Host Redirect		☑
	2	Type of Service Redirect based on Network		☑
	3	Type of Service Redirect based on Host		☑
8	0	Echo Request Ping	☑	
9	0	Router Advertisement	☑	
10	0	Router Solicitation	☑	
11		Time Errors		
	0	Time to Live == 0 during transit		☑
	1	Time to Live == 0 during reassembly		☑
12		Parameter Error		
	0	IP Header Error		☑
	1	Option Field Missing		☑
13	0	Timestamp Request	☑	
14	1	Timestamp Reply	☑	
15	0	Obsolete		
16	0	Obsolete		
17	0	Address Mask Request	☑	
18	0	Address Mask Reply	☑	

a `ttl` value of 64, where `ttl` stands for Time-To-Live and is decremented by 1 each time the packet passes through a router. Therefore the `ttl` value set to 64 allows the packet to route to as many as 64 network hops before the IP packet would be discarded to avoid looping.

I also have setup 192.168.0.10 as a Linux Host running `Tcpdump`. `Tcpdump` is a network monitoring program that captures and records TCP/IP data. `Tcpdump`

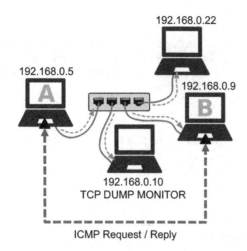

192.168.0.22

192.168.0.5

A

192.168.0.9

B

192.168.0.10
TCP DUMP MONITOR

ICMP Request / Reply

FIGURE 1-7 Simple ICMP Test Network.

is primarily designed to capture packets, however, the program has many options that can also assist in filtering, and performing statistical calculations and provide users with information that can assist in determining the health of their network.

I utilized the following command line to execute the Tcpdump session:

```
$ sudo tcpdump -vv icmp
```

The sudo command pronounced (su "do") allows some (or all) commands to be executed as root provided that the user has the appropriate privilege associated with their account. Tcpdump is the command that we wish to execute as root. The –vv option instructs tcpdump to provide verbose output and finally, the icmp designator instructs tcpdump to only capture icmp packets. The following is the abbreviated packet results captured by the tcpdump command.

TCP Dump Output

Request 1

```
11:10:03.205298 IP (tos 0x0, ttl 64, id 18014, offset 0, flags
[DF], proto ICMP (1), length 84)PythonForensics.local >
192.168.0.9: ICMP echo request, id 4209, seq 1, length 64
```

Reply 1

```
11:10:03.484480 IP (tos 0x0, ttl 64, id 24829, offset 0, flags
[none], proto ICMP (1), length 84)192.168.0.9 >
PythonForensics.local: ICMP echo reply, id 4209, seq 1, length
64
```

Request 2

```
11:10:04.206413 IP (tos 0x0, ttl 64, id 18015, offset 0, flags
[DF], proto ICMP (1), length 84)PythonForensics.local >
192.168.0.9: ICMP echo request, id 4209, seq 2, length 64
```

Reply 2

```
11:10:04.407831 IP (tos 0x0, ttl 64, id 24830, offset 0, flags
[none], proto ICMP (1), length 84)192.168.0.9 >
PythonForensics.local: ICMP echo reply, id 4209, seq 2, length
64
```

_____

.... Skipped for brevity

Request 6

```
11:10:08.210920 IP (tos 0x0, ttl 64, id 18019, offset 0, flags
[DF], proto ICMP (1), length 84)PythonForensics.local >
192.168.0.9: ICMP echo request, id 4209, seq 6, length 64
```

Reply 6

```
11:10:08.408464 IP (tos 0x0, ttl 64, id 24834, offset 0, flags
[none], proto ICMP (1), length 84)192.168.0.9 >
PythonForensics.local: ICMP echo reply, id 4209, seq 6, length
64
```

Now that we have taken a quick tour of Nmap and have a fundamental understanding of a basic `ping` scan we will explore where this book will take us next.

WHAT IS PYTHON PASSIVE NETWORK MAPPING OR P2NMAP?

Simply put, P2NMAP is a method to map networks using only the Python programming language without ever emitting a packet onto the network. In addition, we want our activities to be stealthy and not expose our investigation. This is not for hacking or nefarious purposes as you will see, but in many cases performing these activities without the perpetrators knowledge is important, especially when that perpetrator is an insider.

There are several advantages and some disadvantages of this method. Table 1-2 defines some of these advantages and disadvantages.

Table 1-2 Advantages and Dis-Advantages of P2NMAP

Advantages	Disadvantages
■ Zero overhead or impact on the network itself. This can be very important especially within critical infrastructure environments, where activity scanning technologies can disrupt operations.	■ The time to compile a complete map of the network may take longer, although providing a more thorough view of the environment.
■ The ability to uncover hosts and services that are unknown or are missed by active scanning methods.	■ It is more difficult to identify details such as specific operating systems, hardware types and vulnerabilities.
■ Identify behaviors that are potentially dangerous, hostile, nefarious or outside of defined policies.	
■ P2NMAP provides a full motion video in comparison with the snapshot approach that most active scanning methods provide.	
■ P2NMAP provides an extensible framework where users can add new capabilities and extend behaviors using one of the most popular and easy to learn programming environments.	

The Common Vulnerabilities and Exposure (CVE-2014-016) vulnerability (commonly referred to as "Heartbleed") may be the longest running zero day vulnerability to date. It is important to note, that Heartbleed is NOT a vulnerability of the SSL protocol in general, but rather an example of an implementation bug. Once discovered, it has taken months to fully identify impacted systems, and even longer to remediate a solution. One of the reasons this is so is because to fully identify all the impacted systems, modern vulnerability scanners have to test every IP address and every possible port running on each of those systems. It is simply not enough to scan for common OpenSSL ports and then test for the vulnerability. Thousands of applications and services use OpenSSL and many do not use standard ports like 443.

When scanning for these applications and services the expectation of the scanners is that:

1. All the systems are powered on
2. The scanners have visibility and are not blocked by firewalls or guards
3. The scanning operations themselves won't disrupt operations
4. The vulnerable services are in fact running
5. The vulnerable services are properly responding to the probes.

That is a lot of assumptions. In addition, if those systems are running inside a critical infra-structure environment good luck in convincing the operators to let you start wildly scanning every IP address and every port. Instead a more sanguine approach is to passively monitor these environments with zero danger in causing harm and a greater chance of identifying the full range of systems impacted by Heartbleed. You may say this might take weeks or longer to accomplish using a passive approach. However, ask the real operators of these environ-ments, how long it took to actively scan these environments, how many scans were neces-sary, how many times systems and operations were disrupted and you will find, as the saying goes, that "discretion is the better part of valor".

WHY DOES THIS METHOD CAST A LARGER NET?

The simple answer is that you will find important and undeniable facts about how your network and environment is operating. By passively mapping the behavior of your network you will know, depending upon how long you monitor, every IP address that has touched the environment, what and where in the world they have touched, how often they have communicated, and at what time of day or night were they communicating. This can only be accomplished by patiently mapping these behaviors over time.

Much like cartography which is described as both the art and science of map making, network mapping requires the same discipline, patience and consistency. Unlike cartography, however, where maps are re-drawn every 50-100 years, the maps of our digital network can change dramatically in just days.

You can see the contrast between a modern network map and a cartographer's map in Figure 1-8 and Figure 1-9, respectively.

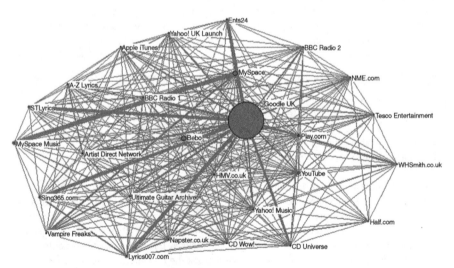

Source: Hitwise UK, October 2006.

Software Credit: Borgatti, S.P., Everett, M.G. and Freeman L.C. 2002, Ucinet for Windows: Software for Social Network Analysis. Harvard, MA: Analytic Technologies.

FIGURE 1-8 Social Network Map.

FIGURE 1-9 Fra Mauro World Map circa 1480 AD.

HOW CAN ACTIVE NETWORK MAPPING ACTUALLY HURT YOU?

Active Network Mapping has several specific impacts:

1. Active network mapping behavior mimics hostile or hacking activity and can cause intrusion prevention systems to react to counter the actions.
2. Host based sensors can also identify these behaviors as hostile and react to the behavior and create outages.
3. Active scanning activities place significant load on the network, servers, routers and network devices.
4. Errors in setting up the scanners, (for example scanning improper IP addresses ranges), can inadvertently impact adjacent networks. If the resulting scan causes damage or outages to those networks, operators of the scanners can be liable.

One of my favorite examples of this comes from a release by Hewlett Packard in the midst of the discovery of the Heartbleed vulnerability:

> "HP Integrated Lights-Out products (iLO, iLO 2, iLO 3, iLO 4) do not use the OpenSSL library and are NOT exposed to the CVE-2014-0160 vulnerability (now known as "Heartbleed") .... However, there is a bug in these libraries that will cause first-generation iLO and iLO 2 devices to enter a live lockup situation when a vulnerability scanner runs to check

for the Heartbleed vulnerability." *http://h20566.www2.hp.com/portal/site/ hpsc/template.PAGE/public/kb/docDisplay?docId=emr_na-c04249852-1&ac. admitted=1406398999314.876444892.199480143*

The point is that by merely scanning these systems for the Heartbleed vulnerability you can literally shut the lights off.

ORGANIZATION OF THE BOOK

In order to quickly address P2NMAP and get you started using, expanding and developing new innovations in passive network mapping, I have arranged the book to get to the point quickly. I would also like to provide detailed explanation of each step, script program and method, thus leaving nothing unexplored.

I want these processes to be easily usable by novice and expert users, students, academics, practitioners, programmers, incident response teams and those wanting to learn about both Python and network investigation as the same time. I always have found learning a new programming language or environment is much more fun if there is a problem to solve first.

In Chapter 2, I explain what you don't know about your network - and more importantly, why you need to know it and why it is important. Also, I look at who is touching your network, and from where. Why should you be concerned about this?

Chapter 3 focuses on how to capture network packets with Python and some special tools. We also look at how you can efficiently store, index and manage what you capture. Most importantly, I discuss how you can do this silently.

Chapters 4 and 5 tackle the analysis of what we have captured, how to make sense of it and how to create an extensible toolkit. This toolkit can be freely used, shared, evolved and also includes opportunities for you to participate in the future expansion.

Chapter 6 takes a look at future opportunities and outlines next steps for P2NMAP.

Finally, each chapter includes a summary of topics covered, challenge problems and review questions making the book suitable for use in college and university academic environments.

REVIEW

In this chapter we quickly examined Nmap and the basic method of scanning and mapping a simple network. We examined the ICMP protocol and demonstrated how ICMP Requests and Reply make up the ping operation that can identify IP addresses on your network. Through this process we showed how many devices not just computers are on your network and do respond to this door-rattling exercise. Next, I provided you with a quick overview definition of what P2NMAP is, and what some of the advantages and disadvantages to this approach are. I also took a look at why passive mapping can be safer and more thorough method for network mapping. Finally, we examined some ways that active mapping can actually be dangerous.

SUMMARY QUESTIONS

1. What are the fundamental differences between active and passive network mapping?
2. What other specific harm could active network mapping cause and/or what regulatory policies could be impacted?
3. What advantages or disadvantages could be caused by passively mapping networks?
4. What benefits and/or limitations do you think choosing a language like Python might pose when applied to network mapping?

References

Nmap Security Scanner, http://nmap.org

Zenmap the official Nmap Security Scanner Graphical User Interface, http://nmap.org/zenmap/

The official web site of *tcpdump*, http://tcpdump.org

## CHAPTER 2

What You DON'T Know About Your Network

"Knowledge speaks, but wisdom listens."

Jimi Hendrix

WHAT'S RUNNING ON YOUR NETWORK MIGHT SURPRISE YOU

Modern environments boast massive infrastructures and sophisticated security technologies designed to keep the bad guys out.

What if the bad guys are already in?

Today, the defensive technology mix includes traditional firewalls, application firewalls, a demilitarized zone (DMZ), virtual private networks (VPN), anti-virus, anti-spyware, patch management infrastructures, content filters, host and network data leak protection (DLP), specialized privilege guards and security event and incident management (SEIM) solutions. Unfortunately, these systems and technologies do little to protect against new threats or hidden vulnerabilities that exist within the environment they protect. In some cases, they exist within the security solutions themselves!

In addition, the solutions today bear resemblance and similar weaknesses to those created by the French Minister of War, Andre Maginot, who in the 1930's created fortifications to protect France from a German invasion. Much like the Maginot line (see figure 2-1), modern cyber security solutions provide great protection against a direct attack, but can be circumvented by insiders through the exploitation of unknown vulnerabilities, via new attack vectors, by means of social engineering activities and can be infiltrated due to lack of deep understanding of one's own environment.

Big vs. Little

It turns out that many smaller organizations are more difficult to penetrate due to the fact that the environment is better understood by both the Information

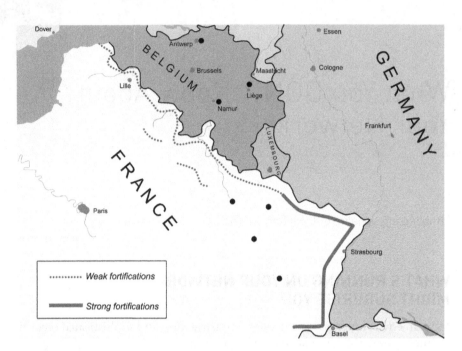

FIGURE 2-1 Map the Maginot Line.

Technology (IT) teams and the Cyber Security teams that protect them. Larger organizations in many cases have undergone numerous mergers and acquisitions along with the melding of information systems. They have also been around longer and likely employ legacy technologies, or have systems operating throughout their network that have simply been forgotten and are running services that are vulnerable.

The following statement is critically important....

> The more you know about your environment, the better you can **protect** your assets, the easier you can **detect** anomalous activity, and the faster you can **react** to new attacks and vulnerabilities.

We Care About What's Running on Our Systems

This might seem obvious as you read this, but you are likely to be surprised by systems and services that are operating on your network. We tend to think only about servers and desktop workstations, since our view of the world is that this is where the information is created, accessed and utilized. Obviously, our infrastructures are changing and what is running or attached to our network is also evolving. Let's just take a look at just a small list of devices and systems we need to be concerned about today (I have purposely left out Servers and Desktop Workstations from the list):

- Android phones and tablets
- iOS phones and tablets
- Windows phones and tablets
- Blackberry phones and tablets
- Printers and multifunction devices (print, scan, fax)
- Copiers and Biz Centers
- Voice Over Internet Protocol (VOIP) systems
- Security cameras
- Internet radios
- Handheld personal cameras
- Near Field Communication Devices (NFC)
- Conference room phones
- Wearable technologies (fitness, surveillance see Figures 2-2–2-4)

Why Do We Care?

At the end of the day, these are all computers at their core with access to networks, the Internet and possibly your corporate infrastructure and information. The questions are:

1. Can you identify them on your network?
2. Do you know where they are located?
3. What data do they have access to?
4. Most importantly, what is the risk and potential impact they pose if compromised?

FIGURE 2-2 Wearable Camera Glasses.

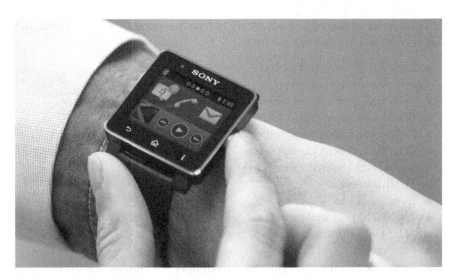

FIGURE 2-3 Smart Watches.

FIGURE 2-4 Wearable Fitness Devices.

The other important aspect of the mobile, wireless, Bluetooth, wearables and NFC devices is that they tend to leave very temporal footprints. Meaning that traditional active network mapping methods may be ineffective in detecting their presence or tracking their behaviors.

Based on this brief introduction, you can see that there are significant advantages to having a firm understanding of the devices that should be attached to our networks, whether these devices are servers, workstations or mobile devices. Think of this as home-field advantage, by understanding what should be operating on your network it becomes easier to identify those devices that shouldn't be there.

As I demonstrated in Chapter 1, actively identifying devices on a network using NMAP quickly provides information about the obvious suspects. What we are looking for here are those devices that operate either in a temporal fashion or are purposely stealthy. Approaching the problem from a passive point view is different in that we have to wait for devices to reveal their presence by actively participating.

Once again we will turn to `tcpdump` to demonstrate some of the ways to capture packets in a passive manner. You might realize that I can do the same thing with Wireshark or a host of other proprietary toolsets. However, one of the problems with this approach is that in order to capture packets at the kernel level, you must be operating at a very high privilege level, and using complex and far-reaching security tools to do so is risky business. Thus my approach throughout the book will be to use simple well-known open-source technologies to perform operations at high levels of privilege. In this way we can limit the need to provide root privilege to only those processes that are absolutely necessary. Likewise our analysis tools (after we have captured the necessary packet samples) can and should operate at a user level.

A Quick Demonstration

Let's answer the following simple question. What computers on my network are hitting remote web servers? To keep things simple, I want to capture only traffic that has a destination address of Port 80. To demonstrate this, I captured some traffic off my home network with `tcpdump` using the following Linux/Unix commands:

First, I placed my eth0 adapter into promiscuous mode.

```
$ sudo ifconfig eth0 promisc
```

Translating the command

sudo:	Execute the command with super user privilege
ifconfig	Linux `ifconfig` command
eth0:	Specify the Ethernet adapter I wish to set
promisc:	Set eth0 in promiscuous mode

After completion of the command we can check the results by running ifconfig. As you can see the eth0 adapter is now running in promiscuous multicast mode

$ **ifconfig eth0**

```
eth0      Link encap:Ethernet  HWaddr 00:1e:8c:b7:6d:64

          inet6 addr: fe80::21e:8cff:feb7:6d64/64 Scope:Link

          UP BROADCAST RUNNING PROMISC MULTICAST

          MTU:1500  Metric:1

          RX packets:43842 errors:0 dropped:108

          overruns:0 frame:0

          TX packets:33 errors:0 dropped:0 overruns:0 carrier:0

          collisions:0 txqueuelen:1000

          RX bytes:4981889 (4.9 MB)   TX bytes:5723 (5.7 KB)
```

Next, I use the tcpdump command to collect any packets originating from source port 80.

$ **sudo tcpdump -i eth0 -n src port 80**

Translating the command:

sudo:	Run the command with super user privilege
tcpdump:	The command we wish to execute at privilege
-i eth0:	Utilize the Ethernet 0 adapter to perform the capture
-n:	Do not resolve IP address to name
src port 80:	only capture packets that have a source port of 80

As a result the command returns a barrage of data. I have snipped out the redundant entries.

```
16:37:06.559388 IP 50.62.120.26.80 > 192.168.0.22.48637: Flags [.], seq

1:1461, ack 505, win 31, length 1460

16:37:06.560713 IP 50.62.120.26.80 > 192.168.0.22.48637: Flags [.], seq

1461:2921, ack 505, win 31, length 1460

<...SNIPPED...>
```

```
16:37:53.787370 IP 108.160.165.54.80 > 192.168.0.22.48532: Flags [P.], seq

380428656:380428835, ack 1424003206, win 31624, length 179

16:37:53.889243 IP 108.160.165.54.80 > 192.168.0.22.48532: Flags [.], ack

360, win 32696, length 0

16:37:59.812185 IP 173.194.37.84.80 > 192.168.0.22.48644: Flags [.], ack

1424, win 361, options [nop,nop,sack 1 {1423:1424}], length 0

<...SNIPPED...>

16:38:09.668759 IP 23.52.91.27.80 > 192.168.0.22.48660: Flags [.], ack 445,

win 490, length 0

16:38:09.670682 IP 23.52.91.27.80 > 192.168.0.22.48660: Flags [.], seq

1:1461, ack 445, win 490, length 1460

16:38:09.670758 IP 23.52.91.27.80 > 192.168.0.22.48660: Flags [P.], seq

1461:2244, ack 445, win 490, length 783

<...SNIPPED...>
```

This results in the following <u>unique</u> values from a network mapping point of view

Table 2-1 Manually Identified Unique Values

Server IP	Client IP	Source Port	Destination Port
50.62.120.26	192.168.0.22	80	48637
108.160.165.54	192.168.0.22	80	48532
23.52.91.27	192.168.0.22	80	48660

How to Do This in Python?

Continuing with the theme of keeping this simple with an eye on passive network mapping, how might we approach this same solution in Python? I will add the ability to automatically generate a unique list of the Server / Client interactions over Port 443.

The script has two basic parts,

1. The Main program that:
   a. Sets up the network interface in promiscuous mode
   b. Opens a raw socket
   c. Listens and reads packets from the raw socket
   d. Calls the `PacketExtractor()` function to decode the packet
   e. Updates a list with packets that meet our port criteria
   f. Once the maximum number of packets are collected a unique list is generated
2. The `PacketExtractor()` function that:
   a. Extracts the IP Header
   b. Extracts the TCP Header
   c. Obtains the Source and Destination IP Addresses
   d. Obtains the Source and Destinations Port Numbers
   e. Makes an educated guess as to the Server vs. Client
   f. Returns a list containing ServerIP, ClientIP, ServerPort

```
# Python Script to Map Activity on a single port
# Running on Linux

# Import Standard Library Modules

import socket            # network interface library used for raw sockets
import os                # operating system functions i.e. file I/o
import sys               # system level functions i.e. exit()
from struct import *     # Handle Strings as Binary Data

# Constants

PROTOCOL_TCP = 6         # TCP Protocol for IP Layer

# PacketExtractor
#
# Purpose: Extracts fields from the IP and TCP Header
#
# Input:    packet:      buffer from socket.recvfrom() method
# Output:   list:        serverIP, clientIP, serverPort
#

def PacketExtractor(packet):

    #Strip off the first 20 characters for the ip header
    stripPacket = packet[0:20]

    #now unpack them
    ipHeaderTuple = unpack('!BBHHHBBH4s4s' , stripPacket)
```

```
# unpack returns a tuple, for illustration I will extract
# each individual values
                                         # Field Contents
verLen        = ipHeaderTuple[0]         # Field 0: Version and Length
TOS           = ipHeaderTuple[1]         # Field 1: Type of Service
packetLength  = ipHeaderTuple[2]         # Field 2: Packet Length
packetID      = ipHeaderTuple[3]         # Field 3: Identification
flagFrag      = ipHeaderTuple[4]         # Field 4: Flags/Fragment Offset
RES           = (flagFrag >> 15) & 0x01  # Reserved
DF            = (flagFrag >> 14) & 0x01  # Don't Fragment
MF            = (flagFrag >> 13) & 0x01  # More Fragments
timeToLive    = ipHeaderTuple[5]         # Field 5: Time to Live (TTL)
protocol      = ipHeaderTuple[6]         # Field 6: Protocol Number
checkSum      = ipHeaderTuple[7]         # Field 7: Header Checksum
sourceIP      = ipHeaderTuple[8]         # Field 8: Source IP
destIP        = ipHeaderTuple[9]         # Field 9: Destination IP

# Calculate / Convert extracted values

version       = verLen >> 4      # Upper Nibble is the version Number
length        = verLen & 0x0F    # Lower Nibble represents the size
ipHdrLength   = length * 4       # Calculate the header length in bytes

# covert the source and destination address to dotted notation strings

sourceAddress      = socket.inet_ntoa(sourceIP);
destinationAddress = socket.inet_ntoa(destIP);

if protocol == PROTOCOL_TCP:

    stripTCPHeader = packet[ipHdrLength:ipHdrLength+20]

    # unpack returns a tuple, for illustration I will extract
    # each individual values using the unpack() function

    tcpHeaderBuffer = unpack('!HHLLBBHHH' , stripTCPHeader)

    sourcePort           = tcpHeaderBuffer[0]
    destinationPort      = tcpHeaderBuffer[1]
    sequenceNumber       = tcpHeaderBuffer[2]
    acknowledgement      = tcpHeaderBuffer[3]
    dataOffsetandReserve = tcpHeaderBuffer[4]
    tcpHeaderLength      = (dataOffsetandReserve >> 4) * 4
    flags                = tcpHeaderBuffer[5]
    FIN                  = flags & 0x01
    SYN                  = (flags >> 1) & 0x01
    RST                  = (flags >> 2) & 0x01
    PSH                  = (flags >> 3) & 0x01
    ACK                  = (flags >> 4) & 0x01
    URG                  = (flags >> 5) & 0x01
    ECE                  = (flags >> 6) & 0x01
```

```
        CWR                   = (flags >> 7) & 0x01
        windowSize            = tcpHeaderBuffer[6]
        tcpChecksum           = tcpHeaderBuffer[7]
        urgentPointer         = tcpHeaderBuffer[8]

        if sourcePort < 1024:
            serverIP   = sourceAddress
            clientIP   = destinationAddress
            serverPort = sourcePort
        elif destinationPort < 1024:
            serverIP   = destinationAddress
            clientIP   = sourceAddress
            serverPort = destinationPort
        else:
            serverIP   = "Filter"
            clientIP   = "Filter"
            serverPort = "Filter"

        return([serverIP, clientIP, serverPort], [SYN, serverIP, TOS,
timeToLive, DF, windowSize])
    else:
        return(["Filter", "Filter", "Filter"], [NULL, Null, Null, Null])

# ------------ MAIN SCRIPT STARTS HERE -----------------

if __name__ == '__main__':

    # Note script must be run in superuser mode
    # i.e. sudo python ..

    # Enable Promiscious Mode on the NIC
    # Make a system call
    # Note: Linux Based

    ret =  os.system("ifconfig eth0 promisc")

    # If successful, then continue
    if ret == 0:

        print "eth0 configured in promiscous mode"

        # create a new socket using the python socket module
        # AF_INET     : Address Family Internet
        # SOCK_RAW    : A raw protocol at the network layer
        # IPPROTO_TCP : Specifies the socket transport layer is TCP

        # Attempt to open the socket
        try:
            mySocket = socket.socket(socket.AF_INET, socket.SOCK_RAW,
socket.IPPROTO_TCP)
```

```
        # if successful post the result
        print "Raw Socket Open"
except:
        # if socket  fails
        print "Raw Socket Open Failed"
        sys.exit()


# create a list to hold the results from the packet capture
# We wil only save Server IP, Client IP, Server Port
# for this example.  Note we will be making and educated guess as to
# differentiate Server vs. Client

ipObservations = []
osObservations = []


# Capture a maximum of 500 observations
maxObservations = 500

# Port filter set to port 443
# TCP Port 443 is defined as the http protocol over TLS/SSL

portValue = 443

try:

    while maxObservations > 0:

        # attempt receive (this call is synchronous, and will wait)
        recvBuffer, addr = mySocket.recvfrom(255)

        # decode the received packet
        # call the local packet extract function above

        content, fingerPrint = PacketExtractor(recvBuffer)

        if content[0] != "Filter":
            # append the results to our list
            # if it matches our port
            if content[2] == portValue:
                ipObservations.append(content)
                maxObservations = maxObservations - 1
                # if the SYN flag is set then
                # record the fingerprint data in osObservations
                if fingerPrint[0] == 1:
                    osObservations.append([fingerPrint[1], \
                                           fingerPrint[2], \
                                           fingerPrint[3], \
                                           fingerPrint[4], \
                                           fingerPrint[5]])
```

```
                       else:
                            # Not our port
                            continue
                  else:
                       # Not a valid packet
                       continue
      except:
         print "socket failure"
         exit()

      # Capture Complete
      # Disable Promiscous Mode
      # using Linux system call
      ret =  os.system("ifconfig eth0 -promisc")

      # Close the Raw Socket
      mySocket.close()

      # Create unique sorted list
      # Next we convert the list into a set to eliminate
      # any duplicate entries
      # then we convert the set back into a list for sorting

      uniqueSrc = set(map(tuple, ipObservations))
      finalList = list(uniqueSrc)
      finalList.sort()

      uniqueFingerprints = set(map(tuple, osObservations))
      finalFingerPrintList = list(uniqueFingerprints)
      finalFingerPrintList.sort()

      # Print out the unique combinations
      print "Unique Packets"
      for packet in finalList:
            print packet
      print "Unique Fingerprints"
      for osFinger in finalFingerPrintList:
            print osFinger
else:
      print 'Promiscious Mode not Set'
```

Sample Program Output

```
eth0 configured in promiscuous mode

Raw Socket Open

Server              Client         Port
Unique Packets
('173.194.37.62', '192.168.0.13', 443)
('199.16.156.241', '192.168.0.13',443)
('199.16.156.52', '192.168.0.13', 443)
('23.235.39.223', '192.168.0.13', 443)
('23.253.135.79', '192.168.0.13', 443)
('23.78.213.231', '192.168.0.13', 443)
('54.192.160.200','192.168.0.13', 443)
('64.233.185.132','192.168.0.13', 443)
('64.233.185.95', '192.168.0.13', 443)
('66.153.250.212','192.168.0.13', 443)
('66.153.250.240','192.168.0.13', 443)
('66.153.250.241','192.168.0.13', 443)
('69.172.216.111','192.168.0.13', 443)
('74.125.137.132','192.168.0.13', 443)
('74.125.196.154','192.168.0.13', 443)
('74.125.196.99', '192.168.0.13', 443)
('93.184.216.146','192.168.0.13', 443)

Unique Fingerprints

Server              TOS   TTL   DF   Window Size
('23.235.39.223',    0,   53,   1,     14480)
('23.253.135.79',    0,   50,   1,     14480)
('64.233.185.132',   0,   42,   0,     42540)
('64.233.185.95',    0,   42,   0,     42540)
('66.153.250.240',   0,   57,   0,     28960)
('66.153.250.241',   0,   57,   0,     28960)
('69.172.216.111',   0,   47,   1,     14480)
('74.125.137.132',   0,   46,   0,     42540)
```

As you can see from this example, it is relatively straight forward to create a simple controlled traffic capture Python script and begin to map simple behaviors on the network. This capture then can process the captured data and identify specific hosts and services they support.

A couple special notes regarding this script.

1. This is a Linux only implementation

2. The Script needs to be run with super user privilege
   ```
   $ sudo python capture443.py
   ```
3. The advantage over using `tcpdump` or Wireshark relates to:
   a. Finer grained control over Super User activity
   b. The simplicity of the operation
   c. The ability to target specific results

OS FINGERPRINTING

I wanted to introduce the concept of OS Fingerprinting up front, since much discussion that surrounds Network Mapping attempts to identify the Operating System that is running behind a particular IP address. This process can be more difficult using passive methods, however it is still possible to make solid arguments for a particular OS. Our focus in the coming chapters is to craft scripts that will ensure that we capture and interpret traffic and fill out the IP range, observe and identify port / service activity and provide clear information regarding what insiders and outsiders are doing.

OS Fingerprinting Using TCP/IP Default Header Values

Several well-known attributes exist for gathering information about the OS executing behind each IP address that we are passively watching. They include:

Table 2-2 Common OS Fingerprinting Fields

IP Header	Defined
TTL	Time to Live
TOS	Type of Service
DF	Don't Fragment Flag
TCP Header	**Defined**
Window	Window Size

> Note, these values are only valuable when the SYN flag is set for a specific TCP packet. You will notice in the capture443.py script, I painstakingly extracted the TTL, TOS, DF from the IP Header and I extract Window Size from the TCP Header. I also create a unique list of the observed fingerprinting values. This script then can be used to record these notable header fields in order to build a more comprehensive "observed" OS fingerprints.

Based on observations from a plethora of sources, Table 2-3 provides a snapshot of observed values that can provide insight to enable fingerprinting an OS. This fingerprinting process is virtually the same for passive vs active mapping - the

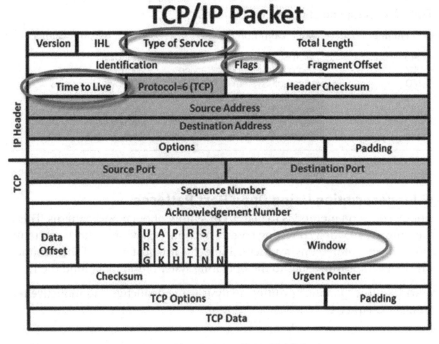

FIGURE 2-5 TCP/IP Header with Key Fingerprinting Fields Highlighted.

only difference being when observing passively, the stimulus must come from normal network traffic, not from artificially generated stimuli.

An educated guess of the OS behind the IP address is possible by creating a comprehensive list of the most common devices. It is important to point out that masking these TCP/IP header fields can be accomplished by those trying to obscure these signatures. Thus it is important to utilize multiple methods:

Table 2-3 Sampling of OS Observed Values

Observed OS	Time to Live Initial Value	Window Size Typical Setting
Linux	64	5840
Open BSD	64	16,384
Solaris	255	8,760
AIX	64	16,384
Windows XP	128	65,535
Windows 2K	128	16,384
Windows 7	128	8,192
Mac OS X	64	65,535

Table 2-4 Sampling of Open Port Patterns

Port Number	Most Common Usage	OS Fingerprint Guess
445	Microsoft Active Directory	Windows
987	Microsoft Sharepoint Service	Windows
1270	Microsoft System Center Operations Manager (SCOM)	Windows
331	Apple OS Server Admin	Mac OS X
660	Mac OS Server Admin	Mac OS X
11111	Remote Configuration Interface	RedHat Linux

OS Fingerprinting Using Open Port Patterns

Another common method is to take an inventory of open port patterns. This is especially useful when collecting passive network behaviors of hosts operating within the monitored environment. Table 2-4 lists just a few of the common ports that can provide clues to the operating system running behind the IP.

We will explore OS Fingerprinting analysis using deductive and inductive reasoning in Chapter 4.

WHAT OPEN PORTS OR SERVICES DON'T YOU KNOW ABOUT?

As was recently seen with the OpenSSL 'Heartbleed' (CVE-2014-0160) and Shellshock (CVE-2014-6271) vulnerabilities, the ability to know what services are operating and on what systems is quite useful. Once again we could use tools like NMAP to discover open ports (at least during the snapshot) with the previously discussed risks. Standard network ports are assigned by the Internet Assigned Numbers Authority (IANA) via the Service Name and Transport Protocol Port Number Registry. Generally (as there is debate) an agreed upon port classification is as follows:

> *Service Ports: 1-1023* are considered <u>well-known ports</u> that represent services that most of us agree to abide by.
> *Service Ports: 1024 to 49151* are recognized as <u>registered ports</u>. They are assigned by IANA upon application and approval.
> *Service Ports: 49152–65535* are considered Dynamic, Private or Ephemeral (i.e. lasting for a short time or transient). For example, ports in this range are commonly used by clients making a connection to a server.

One way to leverage this knowledge of course is to detect traffic originating from, or going to one of these defined ports. By doing so we can deduce services that are running on these hosts and clients that are utilizing them.

In addition to the "agreed upon" port definitions above, organizations such as the SANS Internet Storm Center have created lists of known malicious ports. For example, one compiled list contains default ports utilized by Trojans. Therefore, if you find that one these ports is being probed, it may possibly indicate that someone is attempting to communicate with a Trojan that is running on your network. Thus mapping both the request, and potentially the response to one or more of these ports would be useful in mapping as well.

How is This Useful?

Based on the simple capture443.py script I presented earlier in this chapter, along with the results shown, we could deduce the following:

Local Client 192.168.0.13 has made a secure web page connection to the following servers:

> 199.16.156.201, 23.73.162.234, 66.153.250.229, 66.153.250.234,
> 66.153.250.238, 66.153.250.241, 74.125.137.132, 74.125.137.154,
> 74.125.196.99, 74.125.230.127

This deduction was made based on the following facts:

1. IP address 192.168.0.13 is a Class C private address block. According to RFC 1918, any Class C address in the range 192.168.0.0-192.168.255.255 (which can also be denoted 192.168.0.0/16) should be considered private and non-routable. This means that I cannot directly address any Class C address within that range unless I'm connected to that very same Class C physical network.
2. Each of the other IP addresses can be geographically located. For example, addresses 199.16.156.201 is located in the Mountain View, California area. The IP addresses 66.153.25 are located in South Carolina. Each of these IP addresses communicated with the client over service port 443, which by default is the http protocol running over a secure TLS or SSL connection.

In addition, I could *infer* that client 192.168.0.13 performed a web search that provided a link to the other servers identified. I can make this inference because IP addresses 74.125.137.x belongs to Google, and it is likely that client 192.168.0.13 performed the suggested search using Google.

DEDUCTIVE VS INDUCTIVE REASONING

Deductive reasoning is based on the premise that if the predicates are true, and the logic is sound the conclusion must be valid.

The classic example is

"All men are mortal"
"Socrates was a man"
Therefore: Socrates was mortal

Inductive reasoning, on the other hand, seeks a probable or a likely explanation. A classic example of an inductive argument is:

"All politicians I have met are deceitful"
"I have just met David and he is a politician"
Therefore: David must be deceitful

Much like the inductive argument that was made:

"IP 192.168.0.13 connected to Google"
"Google is the search engine that provides links to other web sites"
Therefore: the subsequent server IP addresses must have come from Google

In both of these cases the likelihood is probable, however unlike the deductive arguments other possible conclusions exist.

In order to perform Passive Network Mapping we will be using both deductive and inductive methods throughout the process. The quality of our arguments, premises, observations and logic will determine how accurate our results will be. Based on that, it will be important to craft these arguments and observations such that they can be improved with time.

Note: Active Network Mapping also uses both methods especially during the process of OS Fingerprinting.

WHO'S TOUCHING YOUR NETWORK?

The next logical question to ask is who is actually touching your network? This includes trusted insiders, employees, IT staff (either in-house or out-sourced), and those outside your direct sphere of control. This doesn't mean just hackers, but can also mean business partners, contract employees, vendors, Internet Service Providers (ISPs), the government, and, of course, your customers. By passively collecting, classifying, analyzing and reasoning about the network activity and open ports, we can glean a tremendous amount of information including:

1. What IP addresses are insiders connecting to?
2. Where are the insiders and outsider located geographically?

3. How often and at what time of day are these services being used? Is this activity normal or abnormal?
4. What IP addresses are outsiders connecting to?
5. Where are these outsiders located geographically?

As you may quickly realize, these questions are more difficult or even in some cases impossible to answer when using active scanning methods, and force direct interaction in response stimulation. In Chapter 4 we will provide scripts that can collect and analyze targeted information that can assist in answering at least some of these questions and provide the foundation for further expanded development.

REVIEW

In Chapter 2, I examined the breadth of devices that may be running on your network that are worth considering. I also discussed their associated risks. I then setup a network capture using Linux and `tcpdump` to capture network packets using promiscuous mode. By manually examining the results I extracted the unique results shown. Next, I developed a Python script that would perform the same type of promiscuous capture, but focused on targeting network activity associated with port 443, which is typically associated with the http protocol over TLS/SSL.

The script also makes an educated guess and converted the typical source IP and destination IP into the more meaningful server vs client characterization. This allowed me to automatically generate the unique list of client server interactions occurring on port 443. Next, I examined the TCP/UDP Port mapping and defined the ranges of well known, registered and ephemeral ports. I then introduced the subtle differences between deductive and inductive reasoning that will be used in future chapters and scripts. Next, I introduced a couple of OS Fingerprinting methods that will be used in Chapter 4. And finally, we examined the additional benefits of Python Passive Network Mapping as applied to behavior of trusted insiders and outsiders.

SUMMARY QUESTIONS

1. What additional network devices will be important to map and identify on our networks and why?
2. How would you generalize the capture443.py script to allow for other targeted captures?
3. Expand the capture443.py script to implement these generalizations.
4. How might you expand capture443.py to create a comprehensive list of unique observed combination of TOS, TTL, DF and Window Size? Then implement the standalone solution.

5. What other OS Fingerprinting methods would be applicable to passive mapping activities.
6. What passive network mapping operations would be best suited for deductive reasoning?
7. What passive network mapping operations would be best suited for inductive reasoning?

Additional Resources

SANS Intrusion Detection FAQ: http://www.sans.org/security-resources/idfaq/oddports.php

IANA – The Internet Assigned Numbers Authority: http://www.iana.org/

TCPDUMP and LIBPCAP: http://www.tcpdump.org/

Introduction to LOGIC, Seventh Edition 1986, by Irving M. Copi ISBN: 0-02-325020-8 McMillan Publishing Company New York New York.

Might I also recommend a good TCP/IP text or two, e.g., Chappell & Tittell, *Guide to TCP/IP* or Stevens, *TCP/IP Illustrated, Vol. 1.* I would also offer my own "An Overview of TCP/IP Protocols and the Internet" at http://www.garykessler.net/library/tcpip.html

## CHAPTER 3

Capturing Network Packets Using Python

"We are drowning in information, but starved for knowledge"

John Naisbitt

SETTING UP A PYTHON PASSIVE NETWORK MAPPING ENVIRONMENT

Chapter 2 provided two initial, (yet incomplete) solutions to promiscuous mode packet capturing. The first used the standard Linux tcpdump command and the second a Python script that captured packets flowing to and from TCP Port 443. The Python script developed in Chapter 2 provides a good foundation for both the capture and extraction of key data from packets traversing the network we are monitoring.

Switch Configuration for Packet Capture

At this point you might be asking how to configure an environment to begin experimenting with packet capturing using these methods. Within most modern networking infrastructures, switches support port mirroring via a Switched Port ANalyzer (SPAN) or Remote Switched Port ANalyzer (RSPAN). For my experimentation and daily use, I'm using a TP-LINK 8 Port Gigabit Easy Smart Switch TL-SG108E as shown in Figure 3-1. I have experimented with many switches and hubs for this purpose, and for a low cost, reliable and easy to configure device, this is the best that I have found so far.

The simplicity of the switch is based on a software application "Easy Smart Configuration Utility", shown in Figure 3-2, that comes with the switch. The configuration utility allows for the configuration of all the features available on the TL-SG108E.

For our purposes, the most important feature is the establishment of a monitoring port that is usable for passively capturing network traffic. Figure 3-3 shows the configuration screen for port monitoring. In this example, I have setup Port 8 to be the monitoring port and ports 2-7 to be monitored. This

CONTENTS

FIGURE 3-1 TL-SG108E 8-Port Gigabit Switch.

means all traffic flowing in or out of ports 2-7 will be available for monitoring on Port 8. Note, I purposely chose to leave port 1 out of the selection. I then connect my sniffing appliance (my Linux computer in this case) to Port 8 of the switch, and I can begin using tcpdump or the Python script developed in Chapter 2 to silently capture network traffic and run experiments.

Computing Resources

Performing packet capture is both processor and memory intensive, so for simple experimentation and demonstration almost any modern platform will due. For the examples in this book, I focus on using Linux and

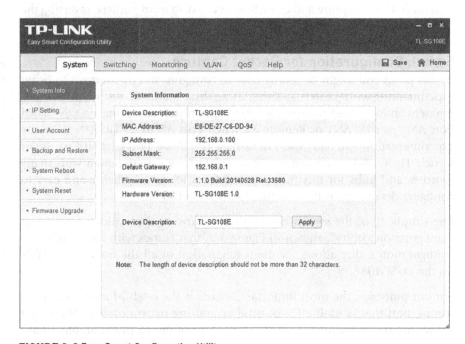

FIGURE 3-2 Easy Smart Configuration Utility.

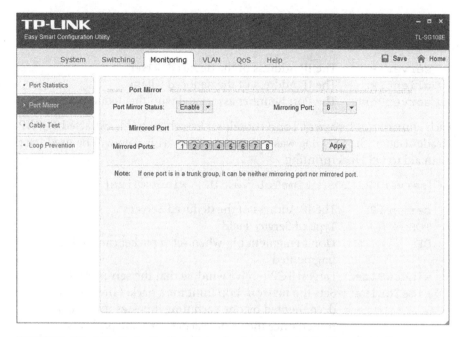

FIGURE 3-3 Port Monitoring Configuration using the Easy Smart Configuration Utility.

Windows. The scripts can be modified to run on Mac as well, but updates to `libcap`, `ifconfig` etc. would be necessary. However, for use in real-world environments where capturing packet data over several days or weeks will require greater considerations, a minimum system would be configured as follows:

- Dual Quad Core Processors 3GHz (in later chapters we will examine multiprocessor separation threading of code)
- 64-128 GB of Memory
- 4 TB of Fixed Storage
- 10 Gbps NIC Card (if the network supports these speeds

Storing Captured Data

The next challenge that we face is the storage of the captured packets, including the definition of what information I need to store. Python offers many internal data structures for this purpose, and if you recall, in Chapter 2, I used Python List Objects to store the captured data:

```
ipObservations = []
osObservations = []
```

Each entry of `ipObservations` List contains:

`[serverIP, clientIP, serverPort]`

`serverIP:`   The IP Address of the deduced Server
`clientIP:`   The IP Address of the deduced Client
`serverPort:`   The Port Number associated with the deduced Server

Each entry of `osObservations` contains a list which holds extracted TCP/IP Header Data if the SYN flag was set for the packet. This data will be used later as an aid to OS Fingerprinting.

`[serverIP, TOS, timeToLive, DF, windowSize]`

`serverIP:`   The IP Address of the deduced Server
`TOS:`   Type of Service Field
`DF:`   Don't Fragment bit; when set, a packet cannot be fragmented
`windowSize:`   Largest TCP receive window that the server can handle.
`timeToLive:`   Sets the network hop limit for a packet life. TTL is decremented by one each time it passes through a router; once the value reaches zero, the packet is discarded to avoid endless looping.

The nice thing about this approach it is quite simple, however, the Python List contains duplicates, and due to the number of packets destined to be collected we want to reduce the size of the packet information we store. So, we must be a little more strategic. In addition, there is some additional information that will be useful to record. Namely, the time that the packets are observed.

Storing the Captured Packets – Python Dictionaries

The question is how to do this without completely saturating the data that we capture? Since the time of each packet would be different if we decide to store the actually time value for each packet, we couldn't remove duplicate `serverIP`, `ClientIP`, `serverPort` packets from our captures. Thus, I have come up with a method of retaining vital time based information regarding each packet, without holding duplicate packets. In addition, this approach will allow for the implementation of Python Dictionaries as the basic storage mechanism.

Python Dictionaries are built-in to the language and thus are quite useful. Fundamentally, Python Dictionaries are Key / Value pairs. Where the Key and Value can be complex types such as Lists or Tuples.

> What is a tuple? A tuple is a sequence of immutable Python objects. Tuples are sequences, much like lists, however tuples can't be changed. The big benefit of tuples is that they are hash-able objects and thus can be used as a Key within a dictionary.

Therefore, let's create a dictionary Key / Value Pair to replace the `ipObserva-tions` List.

```
Key = tuple(serverIP, clientIP, serverPort)
Value =[0,0,0,0,0,0,0,0,0,0,0,0,0,0,0,0,0,0,0,0,0,0,0,0]
```

Each value entry is the number of occurrences of this combination per hour. Note that there are 24 values representing each of the hours of the day. Here is a code snippet that shows how to create a dictionary to do this. Obviously we will be extracting the packet data dynamically and creating the dictionary and key value pairs.

```
ipObserved = {}         # Create an empty dictionary
# Create some fake observed key / value pairs
ipObserved["192.168.0.2", "129.168.0.39", 80] = [0,0,0,0,0,0,0,0,0,0,0,0,0,0,0,0,0,0,0,0,0,0,0,0]
ipObserved["192.168.0.2", "129.168.0.40", 80] = [0,0,0,0,0,0,5,0,0,0,0,0,0,0,0,0,0,2,0,0,0,0,9,0]
ipObserved["192.168.0.2", "129.168.0.41", 80] = [0,0,0,0,0,0,0,0,0,0,0,0,0,0,0,0,0,0,0,0,0,0,0,0]
# Extract a value from a known key
value = ipObserved["192.168.0.2", "129.168.0.40", 80]
# print out the value
print value
# Script output
Value =  [0, 0, 0, 0, 0, 0, 5, 0, 0, 0, 0, 0, 0, 0, 0, 0, 0, 2, 0, 0, 0, 0, 9, 0]
```

`IPObservationDictionary` Class

Approaching the storage of the IP observations in this manner will allow me to keep the size of the storage to a minimum by only recording the unique connection observations (e.g., unique server–client connections). In addition, I will be able to generate histograms of activities based on `serverIP, clientIP` and service type in future chapters based on the hour of the day.

To make this approach re-usable, I will create a class to handle the `IPObservationDictionary`. The class will be simple at first and will be enhanced in later chapters when we begin to process the data collected by the Python Capture process.

```
# ipObservation Class Definition
# and test code

import datetime        # Python Standard Library date and time methods
import pickle          # Python Standard Library pickle methods

#
# Class: IPObservationDictionary
#
# Desc: Handles all methods and properties
#       relating to the IP Observations
#
#
```

```
class IPObservationDictionary:

    # Constructor

    def __init__(self):

        #Attributes of the Object

        self.Dictionary = {}                  # Dictionary to Hold IP Observations

    # Method to Add an observation

    def AddOb(self, key):

        # Obtain the current hour

        now = datetime.datetime.now()
        hour = now.hour

        # Check to see if key is already in the dictionary
        if key in self.Dictionary:

            # If yes, retrieve the current value
            curValue = self.Dictionary[key]

            # Increment the count for the current hour
            curValue[hour-1] = curValue[hour-1] + 1

            # Update the value associated with this key
            self.Dictionary[key] = curValue

        else:
            # if the key doesn't yet exist
            # Create one

            curValue = [0,0,0,0,0,0,0,0,0,0,0,0,0,0,0,0,0,0,0,0,0,0,0]

            # Increment the count for the current hour
            curValue[hour-1] = curValue[hour-1] + 1

            self.Dictionary[key] = curValue

    # Method to retrieve an observation
    # If no observation found return None

    def GetOb(self,key):

        if key in self.Dictionary:
            curValue = self.Dictionary[key]
            return curValue
        else:
            return None

    # Save the Current Observation Dictionary
    # to the specified file
```

```
        def SaveOb(self, fileName):

            with open(fileName, 'wb') as fp:
              pickle.dump(self.Dictionary, fp)

        # Load in and Observation Dictionary
        # from the specified file

        def LoadOb(self, fileName):

            with open(fileName, 'rb') as fp:
                self.Dictionary = pickle.loads(fp.read())

        # Destructor Delete the Object

        def __del__(self):
            print "Closed"

# End IPObservationDictionary Class ======================================


ipOB = IPObservationDictionary()

ipOB.AddOb( ("192.168.0.2", "129.168.0.39", 80) )
ipOB.AddOb( ("192.168.0.2", "129.168.0.41", 80) )
ipOB.AddOb( ("192.168.0.2", "129.168.0.41", 80) )
ipOB.AddOb( ("192.168.0.2", "129.168.0.41", 80) )
ipOB.AddOb( ("192.168.0.2", "129.168.0.41", 80) )
ipOB.AddOb( ("192.168.0.2", "129.168.0.39", 80) )

print "Print out observed values\n"

theValue = ipOB.GetOb( ("192.168.0.2", "129.168.0.41", 80) )
print theValue

theValue = ipOB.GetOb( ("192.168.0.2", "129.168.0.39", 80) )
print theValue

theValue = ipOB.GetOb( ("192.168.0.2", "129.168.0.47", 80) )
print theValue

# Now save the observations to a file
ipOB.SaveOb("SavedObservation.dict")

# Now load the observations from a file
ipOB.LoadOb("SavedObservation.dict")

# Re-check the results are the same

print "Print out observed values after re-loading\n"

theValue = ipOB.GetOb( ("192.168.0.2", "129.168.0.41", 80) )
print theValue

theValue = ipOB.GetOb( ("192.168.0.2", "129.168.0.39", 80) )
print theValue

theValue = ipOB.GetOb( ("192.168.0.2", "129.168.0.47", 80) )
print theValue
```

```
Print out observed values

[0, 0, 0, 0, 0, 0, 0, 0, 0, 0, 0, 0, 0, 0, 0, 0, 0, 0, 4, 0, 0, 0, 0, 0]
[0, 0, 0, 0, 0, 0, 0, 0, 0, 0, 0, 0, 0, 0, 0, 0, 0, 0, 2, 0, 0, 0, 0, 0]
None
Print out observed values after re-loading

[0, 0, 0, 0, 0, 0, 0, 0, 0, 0, 0, 0, 0, 0, 0, 0, 0, 0, 4, 0, 0, 0, 0, 0]
[0, 0, 0, 0, 0, 0, 0, 0, 0, 0, 0, 0, 0, 0, 0, 0, 0, 0, 2, 0, 0, 0, 0, 0]
None
Closed
```

The example and resulting code run verifies that the Dictionary and Class are functioning properly. We have validated each of the class methods:

init: Creates the empty dictionary
AddOb: Adds an observation to the dictionary. If the key does not exist it will create a new entry. If the key exists it will simply add the observation to the proper hour (time slot) for the histogram.
GetOb: Attempts to retrieve and observation based on a key, the key does not exist it return None.
SaveOb: Saves the current Dictionary Object to a file of our choice. This will be useful if we which to periodically save the Dictionary Object to a file.
LoadOb: Loads a previously saved Dictionary object.

OSObservationDictionary **Class**

Very similar to the IPObservationDictionaryClass, this class handles the data storage operations of the operating system observations. These observations include:

The serverIP, TOS, timeToLive, DF, and windowSize, all of which were defined earlier in the chapter.

```
# OSObservation Class Definition
# and test code

import datetime        # Python Standard Library date and time methods
import pickle          # Python Standard Library pickle methods

#
# Class: OSObservationDictionary
#
# Desc: Handles all methods and properties
#       relating to the OSObservations
#
#
```

```python
class OSObservationDictionary:

    # Constructor

    def __init__(self):

        #Attributes of the Object

        self.Dictionary = {}                    # Dictionary to Hold IP Observations

    # Method to Add an observation

    def AddOb(self, key):

        # Obtain the current hour

        now = datetime.datetime.now()
        hour = now.hour

        # Check to see if key is already in the dictionary

        if key in self.Dictionary:

            # If yes, retrieve the current value
            curValue = self.Dictionary[key]

            # Increment the count for the current hour
            curValue[hour-1] = curValue[hour-1] + 1

            # Update the value associated with this key
            self.Dictionary[key] = curValue

        else:
            # if the key doesn't yet exist
            # Create one

            curValue = [0,0,0,0,0,0,0,0,0,0,0,0,0,0,0,0,0,0,0,0,0,0,0,0]

            # Increment the count for the current hour
            curValue[hour-1] = curValue[hour-1] + 1

            self.Dictionary[key] = curValue

    # Method to retrieve an observation
    # If no observation found return None

    def GetOb(self,key):

        if key in self.Dictionary:
            curValue = self.Dictionary[key]
            return curValue
        else:
            return None

    # Save the Current Observation Dictionary
    # to the specified file
```

```python
    def SaveOb(self, fileName):

        with open(fileName, 'wb') as fp:
            pickle.dump(self.Dictionary, fp)

    # Load in and Observation Dictionary
    # from the specified file

    def LoadOb(self, fileName):

        with open(fileName, 'rb') as fp:
            self.Dictionary = pickle.loads(fp.read())

    # Destructor Delete the Object

    def __del__(self):
        print "Closed"

# End OSObservationDictionary Class =====================================


osOB = OSObservationDictionary()

osOB.AddOb( ('23.235.39.223',   0,   53,   1,    14480) )
osOB.AddOb( ('23.253.39.223',   0,   53,   1,    14480) )
osOB.AddOb( ('64.233.185.95',   0,   42,   0,    42540) )
osOB.AddOb( ('64.233.185.95',   0,   42,   0,    42540) )
osOB.AddOb( ('66.153.250.240',  0,   57,   0,    28960) )
osOB.AddOb( ('66.153.250.240',  0,   57,   0,    28960) )


print "Print out observed OS values\n"

theValue = osOB.GetOb( ('23.235.39.223',    0,   53,   1,    14480) )
print theValue

theValue = osOB.GetOb( ('66.153.250.240',   0,   57,   0,    28960) )
print theValue

theValue = osOB.GetOb( ('66.153.250.240',   0,   59,   0,    28960) )
print theValue

# Now save the observations to a file
osOB.SaveOb("SavedOSObservation.dict")

# Now load the observations from a file
osOB.LoadOb("SavedOSObservation.dict")

# Re-check the results are the same

print "Print out observed values after re-loading\n"

theValue = osOB.GetOb( ('23.235.39.223',    0,   53,   1,    14480) )
print theValue

theValue = osOB.GetOb( ('66.153.250.240',   0,   57,   0,    28960) )
print theValue

theValue = osOB.GetOb( ('66.153.250.240',   0,   59,   0,    28960) )
print theValue
```

```
Print out observed OS values

[0, 0, 0, 0, 0, 0, 0, 0, 0, 0, 0, 0, 0, 0, 0, 0, 0, 0, 1, 0, 0, 0, 0, 0]
[0, 0, 0, 0, 0, 0, 0, 0, 0, 0, 0, 0, 0, 0, 0, 0, 0, 0, 2, 0, 0, 0, 0, 0]
None
Print out observed values after re-loading

[0, 0, 0, 0, 0, 0, 0, 0, 0, 0, 0, 0, 0, 0, 0, 0, 0, 0, 1, 0, 0, 0, 0, 0]
[0, 0, 0, 0, 0, 0, 0, 0, 0, 0, 0, 0, 0, 0, 0, 0, 0, 0, 2, 0, 0, 0, 0, 0]
None
Closed
```

THE ART OF THE SILENT CAPTURE

The next step is to enhance our primitive capture script developed in Chapter 2 with the following capabilities:

1. Allow for the capture of TCP or UDP packets specified on the command line
2. Allow for storage of the capture packets into the newly created IPObservationsClass
3. Allow for the storage of the Operating System Observations into the newly created OSObservationsClass
4. Add a PrintOB method to both the IPObservation and OSObservation classes, this will print the contents of the observations
5. Allow the user to specify the time period of the capture
6. Save the results of capture to a file for later analysis

I have covered all of these individual steps and basic capabilities with the exception of the time period for the capture. In order to accomplish this I will introduce the concept of signaling and raise an exception when the time expiries. I will then integrate the specific exception handling operation in the main loop of the script. This requires a few removed steps.

1. I create a class myTimeout that will propagate the exception into the script when the handler fires
2. I create a signal handler that will catch the timeout when the set time expires
3. I need to establish an alarm based on the duration of the capture. (Note capture duration is represented in seconds).
4. Finally, within a try / except block, the specific timeout exception is caught and the perpetual loop is terminated.

```
# Create timeout class to handle capture duration

class myTimeout(Exception):
    pass

# Create a signal handler that raises a timeout event
# when the capture duration is reached

def handler(signum, frame):
    print 'timeout received', signum
    raise myTimeout()

# Set the signal handler to the duraton specified by the user

signal.signal(signal.SIGALRM, handler)
signal.alarm(60)    # set alarm for 60 seconds

try:
    # Create a perpetual loop
    # Inside a try / except block

    while True:
        # do some work
        a = 1+1

# Catch the timeout this breaks the perpetual while loop
# and allows the script to continue

except myTimeout:
            pass
```

PYTHON SOURCE CODE

The final commented P2NMAP capture script shown here includes all the capabilities defined above. I have also included a sample output from the capture script.

I will be creating the actual network map based on the results of this script in following chapters.

```
'''
Copyright (c) 2015 Chet Hosmer, cdh@python-forensics.org

Permission is hereby granted, free of charge, to any person obtaining a copy of this software
and associated documentation files (the "Software"), to deal in the Software without restriction,
including without limitation the rights to use, copy, modify, merge, publish, distribute,
sublicense, and/or sell copies of the Software, and permit persons to whom the Software is
furnished to do so, subject the following condition.
The above copyright notice and this permission notice shall be included in all copies or
substantial portions of the Software.

'''
```

```python
# Python Packet Capture Script
# Python Script to record IP and OS Observations
# For Linux and Windows Platforms

# Import Standard Library Modules

import argparse         # Python Standard Library - Parser for command-line options, arguments
import socket           # network interface library used for raw sockets
import signal           # generation of interrupt signals i.e. timeout
import os               # operating system functions i.e. file I/o
from struct import *    # Handle Strings as Binary Data
import datetime         # Python Standard Library date and time methods
import time             # Python Standard Library time methods
import pickle           # Python Standard Library pickle methods
import platform         # Python Standard Library platform
import sys              # Python Standard Library System Module

# CONSTANTS

PROTOCOL_TCP = 6
PROTOCOL_UDP = 17


#
# Name: ValDirWrite
#
# Desc: Function that will validate a directory path as
#       existing and writable.  Used for argument validation only
#
# Input: a directory path string
#
# Actions:
#               if valid will return the Directory String
#
#               if invalid it will raise an ArgumentTypeError within argparse
#               which will inturn be reported by argparse to the user
#

def ValDirWrite(theDir):

    # Validate the path is a directory
    if not os.path.isdir(theDir):
        raise argparse.ArgumentTypeError('Directory does not exist')

    # Validate the path is writable
    if os.access(theDir, os.W_OK):
        return theDir
    else:
        raise argparse.ArgumentTypeError('Directory is not writable')

#End ValDirWrite =====================================


# Create timeout class to handle capture duration

class myTimeout(Exception):
    pass

# Create a signal handler that raises a timeout event
# when the capture duration is reached
```

```
def handler(signum, frame):
    if VERBOSE:
        print 'Capture Complete', signum
        print

    raise myTimeout()

#
# Class: IPObservationDictionary
#
# Desc: Handles all methods and properties
#       relating to the IPOservations
#
#

class IPObservationDictionary:

    # Constructor

    def __init__(self):

        #Attributes of the Object

        self.Dictionary = {}                 # Dictionary to Hold IP Observations

    # Method to Add an observation

    def AddOb(self, key):

        # Obtain the current hour

        now = datetime.datetime.now()
        hour = now.hour

        # Check to see if key is already in the dictionary

        if key in self.Dictionary:

            # If yes, retrieve the current value
            curValue = self.Dictionary[key]

            # Increment the count for the current hour
            curValue[hour-1] = curValue[hour-1] + 1

            # Update the value associated with this key
            self.Dictionary[key] = curValue

        else:
            # if the key doesn't yet exist
            # Create one

            curValue = [0,0,0,0,0,0,0,0,0,0,0,0,0,0,0,0,0,0,0,0,0,0,0,0]

            # Increment the count for the current hour
            curValue[hour-1] = curValue[hour-1] + 1

            self.Dictionary[key] = curValue

    # Method to retrieve an observation
    # If no observation found return None

    def GetOb(self,key):
```

```python
        if key in self.Dictionary:
            curValue = self.Dictionary[key]
            return curValue
        else:
            return None

# Print the Contents of the Dictionary

# Print the Contents of the Dictionary

def PrintOb(self):
    print "\nIP Observations"
    print "Unique Combinations:    ", str(len(self.Dictionary))
    print

    # Print Heading

    print '                                              ',
    print "|----------------------------------------- Hourly Observations  ---------------
----------------------------------|"
    print '%16s' % "Server",
    print '%16s' % "Client",
    print '%7s'  % "Port",
    print '%5s'  % "Type",

    for i in range(0, 24):
        print ' ',
        print '%02d' % i,
    print

    # Print Contents
    for keys,values in self.Dictionary.items():

        print '%16s' % keys[0],
        print '%16s' % keys[1],
        print '%7s'  % str(keys[2]),
        print '%5s'  % keys[3],

        for i in range(0, 24):
            print '%4s' % str(values[i]),
        print

# Save the Current Observation Dictionary
# to the specified file

def SaveOb(self, fileName):

    with open(fileName, 'wb') as fp:
        pickle.dump(self.Dictionary, fp)

# Load in and Observation Dictionary
# from the specified file

def LoadOb(self, fileName):

    with open(fileName, 'rb') as fp:
        self.Dictionary = pickle.loads(fp.read())

# Destructor Delete the Object

def __del__(self):
    if VERBOSE:
        print "Closed"
```

```
# End IPObservationClass =======================================


#
# Class: OSObservationDictionary
#
# Desc: Handles all methods and properties
#       relating to the OSObservations
#
#

class OSObservationDictionary:

    # Constructor

    def __init__(self):

        #Attributes of the Object

        self.Dictionary = {}                    # Dictionary to Hold IP Observations

    # Method to Add an observation

    def AddOb(self, key):

        # Obtain the current hour

        now = datetime.datetime.now()
        hour = now.hour

        # Check to see if key is already in the dictionary

        if key in self.Dictionary:

            # If yes, retrieve the current value
            curValue = self.Dictionary[key]

            # Increment the count for the current hour
            curValue[hour-1] = curValue[hour-1] + 1

            # Update the value associated with this key
            self.Dictionary[key] = curValue

        else:
            # if the key doesn't yet exist
            # Create one

            curValue = [0,0,0,0,0,0,0,0,0,0,0,0,0,0,0,0,0,0,0,0,0,0,0,0]

            # Increment the count for the current hour
            curValue[hour-1] = curValue[hour-1] + 1

            self.Dictionary[key] = curValue

    # Method to retrieve an observation
    # If no observation found return None

    def GetOb(self,key):

        if key in self.Dictionary:
            curValue = self.Dictionary[key]
```

```python
                return curValue
        else:
            return None

    # Print the Contents of the Dictionary

    def PrintOb(self):

        print "\nOS Observations"
        print "Unique Combinations:    ", str(len(self.Dictionary))
        print


        # Print Heading
        print '                                                  ',
        print "|----------------------------------------- Hourly Observations  ---------------
------------------------------------|"

        print '%16s' % "Server",
        print '%4s'  % "TOS",
        print '%4s'  % "TTL",
        print '%6s'  % "DF",
        print '%7s'  % "Window",

        for i in range(0, 24):
            print ' ',
            print '%02d' % i,
        print

            # Print Contents
        for keys,values in self.Dictionary.items():
            print '%16s' % keys[0],
            print '%4s'  % str(keys[1]),
            print '%4s'  % str(keys[2]),
            print '%6s'  % str(keys[3]),
            print '%7s'  % str(keys[4]),

            for i in range(0, 24):
                print '%4s' % str(values[i]),
            print

    # Save the Current Observation Dictionary
    # to the specified file

    def SaveOb(self, fileName):

        with open(fileName, 'wb') as fp:
            pickle.dump(self.Dictionary, fp)

    # Load in and Observation Dictionary
    # from the specified file

    def LoadOb(self, fileName):

        with open(fileName, 'rb') as fp:
            self.Dictionary = pickle.loads(fp.read())

    # Destructor Delete the Object

    def __del__(self):
        if VERBOSE:
            print "Closed"

# End OSObservationClass ======================================
```

```
# PacketExtractor
#
# Purpose: Extracts fields from the IP and TCP Header
#
# Input:   packet:    buffer from socket.recvfrom() method
# Output:  list:      serverIP, clientIP, serverPort
#

def PacketExtractor(packet):

    if PLATFORM == "LINUX":

        ETH_LEN  = 14      # ETHERNET HDR LENGTH
        IP_LEN   = 20      # IP HEADER    LENGTH
        UDP_LEN  = 8       # UPD HEADER   LENGTH

    elif PLATFORM == "WINDOWS":

        ETH_LEN  = 0       # ETHERNET HDR LENGTH
        IP_LEN   = 20      # IP HEADER    LENGTH
        UDP_LEN  = 8       # UPD HEADER   LENGTH

    else:
        print "Platform not supported"
        quit()

    ethernetHeader=packet[0:IP_LEN]

    #Strip off the first 20 characters for the ip header
    ipHeader = packet[ETH_LEN:ETH_LEN+IP_LEN]

    #now unpack them
    ipHeaderTuple = unpack('!BBHHHBBH4s4s' , ipHeader)

    # unpack returns a tuple, for illustration I will extract
    # each individual values
                                        # Field Contents
    verLen       = ipHeaderTuple[0]     # Field 0: Version and Length
    TOS          = ipHeaderTuple[1]     # Field 1: Type of Service
    packetLength = ipHeaderTuple[2]     # Field 2: Packet Length
    packetID     = ipHeaderTuple[3]     # Field 3: Identification
    flagFrag     = ipHeaderTuple[4]     # Field 4: Flags and Fragment Offset
    RES          = (flagFrag >> 15) & 0x01 # Reserved
    DF           = (flagFrag >> 14) & 0x01 # Don't Fragment
    MF           = (flagFrag >> 13) & 0x01 # More Fragments
    timeToLive   = ipHeaderTuple[5]     # Field 5: Time to Live (TTL)
    protocol     = ipHeaderTuple[6]     # Field 6: Protocol Number
    checkSum     = ipHeaderTuple[7]     # Field 7: Header Checksum
    sourceIP     = ipHeaderTuple[8]     # Field 8: Source IP
    destIP       = ipHeaderTuple[9]     # Field 9: Destination IP

    # Calculate / Convert extracted values

    version    = verLen >> 4        # Upper Nibble is the version Number
    length     = verLen & 0x0F      # Lower Nibble represents the size
    ipHdrLength = length * 4        # Calculate the header length in bytes

    # covert the source and destination address to typical dotted notation strings

    sourceAddress      = socket.inet_ntoa(sourceIP);
    destinationAddress = socket.inet_ntoa(destIP);

    if protocol == PROTOCOL_TCP:
```

```python
        stripTCPHeader = packet[ETH_LEN+ipHdrLength:ipHdrLength+ETH_LEN+IP_LEN]

        # unpack returns a tuple, for illustration I will extract
        # each individual values using the unpack() function

        tcpHeaderBuffer = unpack('!HHLLBBHHH' , stripTCPHeader)

        sourcePort          = tcpHeaderBuffer[0]
        destinationPort     = tcpHeaderBuffer[1]
        sequenceNumber      = tcpHeaderBuffer[2]
        acknowledgement     = tcpHeaderBuffer[3]
        dataOffsetandReserve = tcpHeaderBuffer[4]
        tcpHeaderLength     = (dataOffsetandReserve >> 4) * 4
        flags               = tcpHeaderBuffer[5]
        FIN                 = flags & 0x01
        SYN                 = (flags >> 1) & 0x01
        RST                 = (flags >> 2) & 0x01
        PSH                 = (flags >> 3) & 0x01
        ACK                 = (flags >> 4) & 0x01
        URG                 = (flags >> 5) & 0x01
        ECE                 = (flags >> 6) & 0x01
        CWR                 = (flags >> 7) & 0x01
        windowSize          = tcpHeaderBuffer[6]
        tcpChecksum         = tcpHeaderBuffer[7]
        urgentPointer       = tcpHeaderBuffer[8]

        if sourcePort <= 1024:             # Assume server IP is server
            serverIP  = sourceAddress
            clientIP  = destinationAddress
            serverPort = sourcePort
            status = True
        elif destinationPort <= 1024:      # Assume destination IP is server
            serverIP  = destinationAddress
            clientIP  = sourceAddress
            serverPort = destinationPort
            status = True
        elif sourcePort <= destinationPort: # Assume server IP is server
            serverIP  = sourceAddress
            clientIP  = destinationAddress
            serverPort = sourcePort
            status = True
        elif sourcePort > destinationPort:  # Assume distinatin IP is server
            serverIP  = destinationAddress
            clientIP  = sourceAddress
            serverPort = destinationPort
            status = True
        else:                              # Should never get here
            serverIP  = "FILTER"
            clientIP  = "FILTER"
            serverPort = "FILTER"
            status = False

        return( status, (serverIP, clientIP, serverPort, "TCP"), [SYN, serverIP, TOS, timeToLive, DF, windowSize] )

    elif protocol == PROTOCOL_UDP:

        stripUDPHeader = packet[ETH_LEN+ipHdrLength:ETH_LEN+ipHdrLength+UDP_LEN]

        # unpack returns a tuple, for illustration I will extract
        # each individual values using the unpack() function

        udpHeaderBuffer = unpack('!HHHH' , stripUDPHeader)
```

```
            sourcePort              = udpHeaderBuffer[0]
            destinationPort         = udpHeaderBuffer[1]
            udpLength               = udpHeaderBuffer[2]
            udpChecksum             = udpHeaderBuffer[3]

            if sourcePort <= 1024:                      # Assume server IP is server
                serverIP    = sourceAddress
                clientIP    = destinationAddress
                serverPort = sourcePort
                status = True
            elif destinationPort <= 1024:               # Assume destination IP is server
                serverIP    = destinationAddress
                clientIP    = sourceAddress
                serverPort = destinationPort
                status = True
            elif sourcePort <= destinationPort: # Assume server IP is server
                serverIP    = sourceAddress
                clientIP    = destinationAddress
                serverPort = sourcePort
                status = True
            elif sourcePort > destinationPort:  # Assume distinatin IP is server
                serverIP    = destinationAddress
                clientIP    = sourceAddress
                serverPort = destinationPort
                status = True
            else:                                       # Should never get here
                serverIP    = "FILTER"
                clientIP    = "FILTER"
                serverPort = "FILTER"
                status = False

            return( status, (serverIP, clientIP, serverPort, "UDP"),
["FILTER","FILTER","FILTER","FILTER","FILTER","FILTER"] )
        else:

            return( False, ("Filter", "Filter", "Filter", "FILTER"),
["FILTER","FILTER","FILTER","FILTER","FILTER","FILTER"] )


#
# Class Spinner
#
# Used to display a spinning character on the screen to show progress
#
#
class Spinner:

    # Constructor

    def __init__(self):

        self.symbols = [' |', ' /', ' -', ' \\', ' |', ' \\', ' -', 'END']
        self.curSymbol = 0

        sys.stdout.write("\b\b\b%s " % self.symbols[self.curSymbol])
        sys.stdout.flush()

    def Spin(self):

        if self.symbols[self.curSymbol] == 'END':
            self.curSymbol = 0

        sys.stdout.write("\b\b\b%s " % self.symbols[self.curSymbol])
        sys.stdout.flush()
        self.curSymbol += 1
```

```python
# End Spinner Class

# Main Program Starts Here
#=====================================

if __name__ == '__main__':

    # Setup Argument Parser Object

    parser = argparse.ArgumentParser('P2NMAP-Capture')

    parser.add_argument('-v', '--verbose', help="Display packet details", action='store_true')
    parser.add_argument('-m', '--minutes', help='Capture Duration in minutes',type=int)
    parser.add_argument('-p', '--outPath', type= ValDirWrite, required=True, help="Output
Directory")

    theArgs = parser.parse_args()

    VERBOSE = theArgs.verbose

# Calculate capture duration
captureDuration = theArgs.minutes * 60

try:
    # Note script must be run in superuser mode
    # i.e. sudo python ..

    if platform.system() == "Linux":

        PLATFORM = "LINUX"

        # Enable Promiscuous Mode on the NIC
        # Make a system call
        # Note: Linux Based

        ret =  os.system("ifconfig eth0 promisc")
        if ret != 0:
            print 'Promiscuous Mode not Set'
            quit()

        # create a new socket using the python socket module
        # PF_PACKET   : Specifies Protocol Family Packet Level
        # SOCK_RAW    : Specifies A raw protocol at the network layer
        # socket.htons(0x0800) : Specifies all headers and packets
        #                        : Ethernet and IP, including TCP/UDP etc

        # Attempt to open the socket for capturing raw packets

        rawSocket=socket.socket(socket.PF_PACKET,socket.SOCK_RAW,socket.htons(0x0800))

        # Set the signal handler to the duraton specified by the user

        signal.signal(signal.SIGALRM, handler)
        signal.alarm(captureDuration)

    elif platform.system() == "Windows":

        PLATFORM = "WINDOWS"

        # For the Windows Platform the setup is also different

        # Retreive our our IP Address to bind to
        hostname = socket.gethostname()
        host = socket.gethostbyname(hostname)
```

```
            # Create a rawSocket
            rawSocket = socket.socket(socket.AF_INET, socket.SOCK_RAW, socket.IPPROTO_IP)
            # Set the socket Options
            rawSocket.setsockopt(socket.IPPROTO_IP, socket.IP_HDRINCL, 1)
            # Bind to our host
            rawSocket.bind( (host,0))
            # Set socket to receive all packets
            rawSocket.ioctl(socket.SIO_RCVALL, socket.RCVALL_ON)

            startTime = time.time()
            endTime = startTime + captureDuration

        else:
            print "Platform not supported"
            quit()
    except:
        print "Socket Error"
        quit()

    if VERBOSE:
        print "Network      : Promiscuous Mode"
        print "Sniffer      : Ready: \n"

        # Create a Spinner Object for displaying progress
        obSPIN = Spinner()

    # Create IP and OS observation dictionaires

    ipOB = IPObservationDictionary()
    osOB = OSObservationDictionary()

    # Create a perpetual loop, we will be
    # interrupted by the timeout value only

    packetsCaptured = 0
    try:
        while True:

            # attempt to recieve (this call is synchronous, thus it will wait)
            receivedPacket=rawSocket.recv(65535)

            packetsCaptured += 1              # Count the captured packets

            if VERBOSE:
                # Update the Display
                obSPIN.Spin()

            # decode the received packet
            # call the local packet extract function above

            status, osContent, fingerPrint = PacketExtractor(receivedPacket)

            # If status returns true
            # we can process the results

            if status:

                # Add content to ipObservations

                ipOB.AddOb(osContent)

                if fingerPrint[0] == 1:
                    osContent = tuple(fingerPrint[1:])
                    osOB.AddOb(osContent)

            else:
                # Not a valid packet
                continue
```

```
        if PLATFORM == "WINDOWS":
            if time.time() > endTime:
                raise myTimeout

except myTimeout:
    pass

# Capture Complete

if VERBOSE:

    print "\nTotal Packets Captured: ", str(packetsCaptured)
    print

    ipOB.PrintOb()
    osOB.PrintOb()

    print "\nSaving Observations ext: .ipDict and .osDict"

ipOutFile = datetime.datetime.now().strftime("%Y%m%d-%H%M%S")+".ipDict"
osOutFile = datetime.datetime.now().strftime("%Y%m%d-%H%M%S")+".osDict"

ipOutput = os.path.join(theArgs.outPath, ipOutFile)
osOutput = os.path.join(theArgs.outPath, osOutFile)

ipOB.SaveOb(ipOutput)
osOB.SaveOb(osOutput)

if PLATFORM == "LINUX":
    # Disable Promiscuous Mode on the NIC
    # Make a system call
    # Note: Linux Based

    ret =  os.system("ifconfig eth0 -promisc")

elif PLATFORM == "WINDOWS":
    rawSocket.ioctl(socket.SIO_RCVALL, socket.RCVALL_OFF)

else:
    print "Platform not supported"
    quit()

# Close the Raw Socket
rawSocket.close()
```

Command Line Entry and Execution of P2NMAP-Capture.py

Windows: (note the command prompt must be launched with Administrator Rights:

```
python P2MAP-Capture.py -v -m 2 -p ./
```

Linux:

```
sudo python P2MAP-Capture.py -v -m 2 -p ./
```

```
Network  : Promiscuous Mode
Sniffer  : Ready:


Total Packets Captured:  2195

IP Observations
Unique Combinations:  33
```

Hourly Observations

Server	Client	Type	Port	00	01	02	03	04	05	06	07	08	09	10	11	12	13	14	15	16	17	18	19	20	21	22	23
192.168.0.255	192.168.0.6	UDP	8612	0	0	0	0	0	0	0	0	0	0	0	16	0	0	0	0	0	0	0	0	0	0	0	0
91.189.92.152	192.168.0.19	TCP	80	0	0	0	0	0	0	0	0	0	0	0	17	0	0	0	0	0	0	0	0	0	0	0	0
127.0.0.1	127.0.0.1	UDP	53	0	0	0	0	0	0	0	0	0	0	0	24	0	0	0	0	0	0	0	0	0	0	0	0
192.168.0.11	255.255.255.255	UDP	17500	0	0	0	0	0	0	0	0	0	0	0	3	0	0	0	0	0	0	0	0	0	0	0	0
192.168.0.11	239.255.255.250	UDP	1900	0	0	0	0	0	0	0	0	0	0	0	8	0	0	0	0	0	0	0	0	0	0	0	0
91.189.92.191	192.168.0.14	TCP	80	0	0	0	0	0	0	0	0	0	0	0	1	0	0	0	0	0	0	0	0	0	0	0	0
255.255.255.255	192.168.0.14	UDP	8611	0	0	0	0	0	0	0	0	0	0	0	3	0	0	0	0	0	0	0	0	0	0	0	0
0.0.0.0	255.255.255.255	UDP	68	0	0	0	0	0	0	0	0	0	0	0	6	0	0	0	0	0	0	0	0	0	0	0	0
192.168.0.11	192.168.0.255	UDP	137	0	0	0	0	0	0	0	0	0	0	0	12	0	0	0	0	0	0	0	0	0	0	0	0
239.255.255.250	192.168.0.12	UDP	1900	0	0	0	0	0	0	0	0	0	0	0	1	0	0	0	0	0	0	0	0	0	0	0	0
209.18.47.61	192.168.0.19	UDP	53	0	0	0	0	0	0	0	0	0	0	0	16	0	0	0	0	0	0	0	0	0	0	0	0
192.168.0.5	224.0.0.251	UDP	5353	0	0	0	0	0	0	0	0	0	0	0	2	0	0	0	0	0	0	0	0	0	0	0	0
224.0.0.1	192.168.0.6	UDP	8612	0	0	0	0	0	0	0	0	0	0	0	56	0	0	0	0	0	0	0	0	0	0	0	0
255.255.255.255	192.168.0.14	UDP	8612	0	0	0	0	0	0	0	0	0	0	0	12	0	0	0	0	0	0	0	0	0	0	0	0
239.255.255.250	192.168.0.13	UDP	1900	0	0	0	0	0	0	0	0	0	0	0	12	0	0	0	0	0	0	0	0	0	0	0	0
169.254.7.79	224.0.144.1	UDP	52613	0	0	0	0	0	0	0	0	0	0	0	4	0	0	0	0	0	0	0	0	0	0	0	0
192.168.0.14	255.255.255.255	UDP	17500	0	0	0	0	0	0	0	0	0	0	0	1	0	0	0	0	0	0	0	0	0	0	0	0
192.168.0.6	192.168.0.255	UDP	17500	0	0	0	0	0	0	0	0	0	0	0	4	0	0	0	0	0	0	0	0	0	0	0	0
192.168.0.14	192.168.0.255	UDP	138	0	0	0	0	0	0	0	0	0	0	0	2	0	0	0	0	0	0	0	0	0	0	0	0
239.255.255.250	192.168.0.4	UDP	1900	0	0	0	0	0	0	0	0	0	0	0	1	0	0	0	0	0	0	0	0	0	0	0	0
209.18.47.62	192.168.0.19	UDP	53	0	0	0	0	0	0	0	0	0	0	0	1340	0	0	0	0	0	0	0	0	0	0	0	0
91.189.91.24	192.168.0.19	TCP	80	0	0	0	0	0	0	0	0	0	0	0	4	0	0	0	0	0	0	0	0	0	0	0	0
192.168.0.11	192.168.0.255	UDP	17500	0	0	0	0	0	0	0	0	0	0	0	596	0	0	0	0	0	0	0	0	0	0	0	0
91.189.91.14	192.168.0.19	TCP	80	0	0	0	0	0	0	0	0	0	0	0	3	0	0	0	0	0	0	0	0	0	0	0	0
255.255.255.255	192.168.0.11	UDP	1947	0	0	0	0	0	0	0	0	0	0	0	4	0	0	0	0	0	0	0	0	0	0	0	0
224.0.0.252	192.168.0.11	UDP	5355	0	0	0	0	0	0	0	0	0	0	0	2	0	0	0	0	0	0	0	0	0	0	0	0
239.255.255.250	169.254.7.79	UDP	1900	0	0	0	0	0	0	0	0	0	0	0	4	0	0	0	0	0	0	0	0	0	0	0	0
192.168.0.6	255.255.255.255	UDP	17500	0	0	0	0	0	0	0	0	0	0	0	3	0	0	0	0	0	0	0	0	0	0	0	0
239.255.255.250	192.168.0.18	UDP	1900	0	0	0	0	0	0	0	0	0	0	0	1	0	0	0	0	0	0	0	0	0	0	0	0
239.255.255.250	192.168.0.14	UDP	1900	0	0	0	0	0	0	0	0	0	0	0	3	0	0	0	0	0	0	0	0	0	0	0	0
127.0.0.1	127.0.0.1	TCP	41637	0	0	0	0	0	0	0	0	0	0	0	4	0	0	0	0	0	0	0	0	0	0	0	0
192.168.0.14	255.255.255.255	UDP	17500	0	0	0	0	0	0	0	0	0	0	0	3	0	0	0	0	0	0	0	0	0	0	0	0
192.168.0.255	192.168.0.11	UDP	1947	0	0	0	0	0	0	0	0	0	0	0	3	0	0	0	0	0	0	0	0	0	0	0	0

```
OS Observations
Unique Combinations:  4
```

Hourly Observations

Server	TOS	TTL	DF	Window	00	01	02	03	04	05	06	07	08	09	10	11	12	13	14	15	16	17	18	19	20	21	22	23
91.189.91.14	40	50	1	14480	0	0	0	0	0	0	0	0	0	0	0	1	0	0	0	0	0	0	0	0	0	0	0	0
91.189.92.152	0	48	1	14480	0	0	0	0	0	0	0	0	0	0	0	1	0	0	0	0	0	0	0	0	0	0	0	0
91.189.92.191	0	49	1	5792	0	0	0	0	0	0	0	0	0	0	0	1	0	0	0	0	0	0	0	0	0	0	0	0
91.189.91.24	40	47	1	28960	0	0	0	0	0	0	0	0	0	0	0	1	0	0	0	0	0	0	0	0	0	0	0	0

```
Saving Observations ext: .ipDict and .osDict
Closed
Closed
```

REVIEW

In Chapter 3, we examined the rules of thumb necessary to setup a packet capture environment, including the discussion of switch selection and configuration along with system hardware considerations. Next, we examined the "kind-of" information that is required to collect from network packets that will eventually aid in the passive mapping of a network and operating system fingerprinting. I then considered different Python data types that could dynamically store the packet results, and the Python Dictionary was chosen as the data storage type. Special consideration was given to the construction of these dictionaries in order to eliminate duplicate observations. In addition, I devised a method for including a basic histogram of similar packet occurrence for each unique combination of `Server IP, Server Port and Client IP`. At this point I designed two classes: `IPObservationsDictionary` and `OS-ObservationDictionary` that handle creation, adding, reading, loading, saving and printing of the associated Dictionary. I then revealed the concept of signaling to handle a time based capture of packets. Finally, I combined all these capabilities into a single script to perform packet capture and storage.

SUMMARY QUESTIONS

1. What additional information might be useful for network mapping or OS Fingerprinting to store about each packet without disrupting the reduction of duplicate entries?
2. For packets with both source IP and Destination IP addresses above 1024, what method could be developed to better establish server vs. client identity.
3. How might we filter out specific packet types or IP ranges from our capture in order to reduce the storage requirements?

Additional Resource

O'Connor, T.J., 2013. Violent Python: A Cookbook for Hackers, Forensic Analysts, Penetration Testers and Security Engineers. Elsevier, ISBN-13: 978-1597499576, Chapter 4, Network Traffic Analysis with Python.

Packet Capture Analysis

"All great truths are simple in final analysis, and easily understood; if they are not, they are not great truths."

Napoleon Hill

PACKET CAPTURE ANALYSIS

Now that we have "P2NMAP-Capture.py" in hand, a Python Packet Capture Tool that performs well on both Windows and Linux platforms, along with creating a dictionary of time collected results, we now can perform some useful analysis of the collected data.

As you observed in Chapter 3, the tool produces two output files:

```
02/06/2015   01:24 PM     10,737 20150206-132401.ipDict

02/06/2015   01:24 PM     6,906  20150206-132438.osDict
```

20150206-132401.ipDict contains the Internet Protocol Observations Dictionary, and 20150206-132438.osDict contains the Operating System Observations Dictionary. In this chapter I focus on the analysis of the .ipDict observations.

A key aspect of the P2NMAP approach is to passively monitor network traffic and record the results without ever placing a packet on the network. A second key is to collect data over a period of time, measured in at least hours - if not days. This approach is in direct contrast with active mapping methods that probe network devices, and there are advantages and disadvantages to both methods.

One of the key advantages of the passive approach is to be able to observe the behavior of network devices over the course of days or even weeks and map behaviors of both servers and clients over the period.

CONTENTS

Yet another important aspect of the technical approach is the development of the `ipObservationDictionary` Class. Using a class for this purpose allows us to re-use the class as a starting point for the development of the analysis methods. For example, the class already contains methods to save and load IP Dictionary Files, along with methods to print out the Internet Protocol observations stored in the currently loaded dictionary. By extending the capabilities of the class and the resulting instantiated objects, we can provide a straight-forward method to advance the analysis capabilities now and in the future.

The initial set of methods that are to be added to the `ipObservationDictionary` Class over the capture period include:

1. Load an Observation File
2. Print out all the recorded observations
3. Print the unique list of identified servers along with ports in use
4. Print the unique list of identified clients
5. Print the unique connection list (servers to client) with port details
6. Print 24 hour histogram of activity for each unique server / client connections

In addition, to this base set of analysis items, I have also provided three special lookups to provide additional information for the analyst. They include:

1. Port Number to Port Name Conversion
2. Host Name Lookup based on IP Address (note this requires Internet Access)
3. Country Location based on the IP Address

To access these capabilities I have created a simple menu driven script, P2NMAP-Analyze.py to perform the defined analysis operations. Figure 4-1 depicts the P2NMAP-Analyze.py menu.

In the following sections, I will discuss the operation, implementation and rationale for each menu operation.

SETTING UP OPTIONS FOR ANALYSIS

Before we begin to execute the analysis methods themselves, several options are necessary to set within the interface. They include:

1. Loading an Observation File
2. Directing the Program Output
3. Specifying the Host Lookup Option
4. Specifying the Country Lookup Option

```
========== P2NMAP Analysis Menu ==========

Current Observation File:  test.ipdict

[L]    Load Observation File for Analysis
[O]    Direct Output to File    (Current = Stdout)
[H]    Turn On Host Lookup      (Current = Host Lookup Off)
[C]    Turn On Country Lookup   (Current = Country Lookup Off)
================================================================
[1]    Print Observations       (ALL)
[2]    Print Servers            (Unique)
[3]    Print Clients            (Unique)
[4]    Print Connections        (Unique by Server)
[5]    Print Histogram

[X]    Exit P2NMAP Analysis

Enter Selection:
```

FIGURE 4-1 P2NMAP Analysis Menu.

Loading an Observation File

Loading an observation file is quite straight-forward. During the capture process I saved the ipDict file using Python's built in Pickle Module. The Python Standard Library module, *pickle* provides the ability to pickle and un-pickle an object, where pickling converts any Python object such as a list, set, dictionary or any other object into a character stream. The character stream contains all the information that would be necessary to reconstruct the object within another Python script. This is exactly what we wanted to do as I have de-coupled the capture and analysis capabilities of P2NMAP. Since I wanted to provide a completely Python-based solution for Passive Network Mapping, I separated the operations in this manner.

> If you wanted to use a .pcap file or other packet capture method, you would simply extract data from the .pcap file and create a Python dictionary object. Then the P2NMAP-Analysis.py script could then be applied to the resulting pickled dictionary file. Note: See Chapter 5 for a script that will accomplish this process.

The only two methods that are necessary to accomplish this are:

```
pickle.dump(self.Dictionary, fp)           # Write the Object out to a File

self.Dictionary = pickle.loads(fp.read())  # Read the Object in from a File
```

where `self.Dictionary` is the Dictionary object I wish to save or load. The

object `fp` is the File Pointer to either the output or input file.

I added the following method to the class `IPObservationDictionary` as shown below:

```
# Load in an Observation Dictionary
# from the specified file

def LoadOb(self, fileName):
try:
    with open(fileName, 'rb') as fp:
        self.Dictionary = pickle.loads(fp.read())
        self.observationFileName = fileName
        self.observationsLoaded  = True
except:
    print "Loading Observations - Failed"
    self.observationsLoaded = False
    self.observationFileName = ""
```

If the method is successful it sets the object attributes:

- `self.observationsLoaded` to True
- `self.observationFileName` to the file name that was loaded.

These two attributes are used by other methods within the class `IPObservationDictionary`.

However, if the load fails, the `self.observationsLoaded` attribute is set to False and the `self.observationFileName` is set to blank. In addition an error message is displayed to the user.

As you will see during the operation of the script, no other operations will be available to the user until a valid observation file is successfully loaded.

Direct Program Output

One of the questions that I get quite often is: How do I use the same print statement to direct output to either 'standard out' or to a file. The problem with using the redirect symbol, ' > ' as shown here....

```
$ python P2NMAP-Analysis.py > results.txt
```

....is that all messages are sent to the results file including prompts, informational and warning messages. This can be solved using the following method in Python:

I create a variable named OUT and set it equal to the result of an open method such as the one shown below. I then preface every print message with `print >> OUT`, and whatever follows is then written directly to the output file, regardless of the complexity. This will ensure that the output file will look exactly like the output that would have been displayed on the screen using 'standard out'.

```
OUT = open("results.txt", 'w+')
```

```
print >> OUT, "This is a message"
```

The question then becomes, how do I then direct the output to 'standard out'?

That turns out to be the easy part if you know your way around the Python Standard Library module. If the OUT variable is global, then by allowing the user to change the variable, the output will be directed to the proper output, in this case either standard out or the file results.txt.

```
OUT = sys.stdout
```

```
print >> OUT, "This is a message"
```

To implement this in the module, I create a toggle allowing the user to change the output direction between 'standard out' and a file. This way, the analyst can review the output on the screen and then once they are satisfied with the results they can toggle and have the function output directed to the file. Note, this is a good technique to use within any forensic related script. Here is the code excerpt that performs the toggle when the user selects the 'O' output option from the menu. Notice that I perform the close method, `OUT.close()` when switching from file output back to STDOUT. This ensures that the file will be closed and all data will be written to the file. Also, I open the output file using "w+", meaning that data will be appended to the results.txt file.

```
    elif menuSelection == 'O':
        if PRINT_STDOUT:
            PRINT_STDOUT = False
            OUT = open("results.txt", 'w+')
        else:
            PRINT_STDOUT = True
            OUT.close()
            OUT = sys.stdout
```

Specifying the Host Lookup Option

One of the important aspects of passive network capture is the mapping of IP addresses to Host Names. This is done using network address translation, in this case from IP address to Host Name. In the spirit of this book (so far), I want to perform this lookup using native Python code and Python Standard Libraries. It turns out that this is quite simple to do, but just a word of warning .... this will take time and Internet access to accomplish. Once again I will use the toggle method within the menu system to provide the user with the option of turning Host Lookup on or off, with the default being Host Lookup is off.

```
elif menuSelection == 'H':

    if HOST_LOOKUP:

        HOST_LOOKUP = False

    else:

        HOST_LOOKUP = True
```

The HOST_LOOKUP variable is then evaluated by each of the analysis methods. If the HOST_LOOKUP is true, then the analysis methods will translate the IP address into the related host name. The code to perform this lookup utilizes the Python Standard Library Module, socket and only requires a single socket call to accomplish this:

```
try:

    # if caller requested hostname lookup

    # perform the lookup, else set name to blank

    if HOST_LOOKUP:

        hostName = socket.gethostbyaddr(serverIP)

    else:

        hostName = ["", "", ""]

except:

    hostName = ""

    continue
```

> It is important to note that the `socket.gethostbyaddr()` returns a triple.
>
> According to the Python Standard Library Reference: "The Triple (hostname, aliaslist, ipaddrlist) where hostname is the primary host name responding to the given ip_address, aliaslist is a (possibly empty) list of alternative host names for the same address, and ipaddrlist is a list of IPv4/v6 addresses for the same interface on the same host (most likely containing only a single address)."

For our application we are only interested in the first element of the triple, the name of the host. If exceptions occur during the call (in other words, the host name could not be associated with a specific IP address), I fill the triple with blanks so when those elements are accessed in the code, they are simply printed as blanks.

Specifying the Country Lookup Option

When investigating server and client IP addresses, one of the typical questions that arises is "Where is the IP located geographically?" In some cases this is difficult to confirm if the server or client are attempting to anonymize their locations, however for most cases the mapping of IP address to a general geographic region is possible.

To handle this specific lookup I'm going to use a Python 3rd Party Library and dataset. The 3rd Party Library is `pygeoip`.

To install the `pygeoip` library within your Python Environment you can use pip. Pip is the most popular Python package management system, and is used to install and manage 3rd party packages written in Python. The `pygeoip` library is installed from the command line; note that the pip package management system must already be installed.

```
$ pip install pygeoip
```

Or

```
C:\> pip install pygeoip
```

Once `pygeoip` is installed, you must also download the latest database from MAXMIND developer website at: http://dev.maxmind.com/geoip/legacy/geolite/

For the examples in this chapter I downloaded the GeoLite Country Binary/ Gzip Version as shown in Figure 4-2. I then unzipped and placed the geo.dat file in my source directory for easy access. Note, I changed the name to geo.dat as the unzip generates GeoIP.dat, this way when I download updates I can keep track of new vs old.

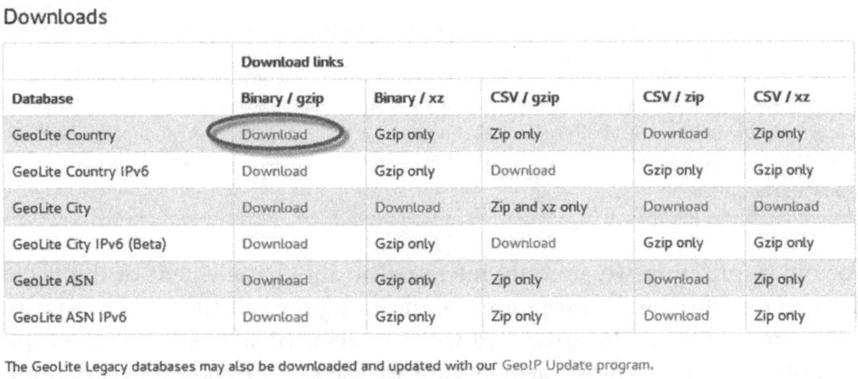

Downloads

	Download links				
Database	Binary / gzip	Binary / xz	CSV / gzip	CSV / zip	CSV / xz
GeoLite Country	Download	Gzip only	Zip only	Download	Zip only
GeoLite Country IPv6	Download	Gzip only	Download	Gzip only	Gzip only
GeoLite City	Download	Download	Zip and xz only	Download	Download
GeoLite City IPv6 (Beta)	Download	Gzip only	Download	Gzip only	Gzip only
GeoLite ASN	Download	Gzip only	Zip only	Download	Zip only
GeoLite ASN IPv6	Download	Gzip only	Zip only	Download	Zip only

The GeoLite Legacy databases may also be downloaded and updated with our GeoIP Update program.

FIGURE 4-2 MAXMIND GeoLite Country Database Binary/Gzip Version.

Following the instructions on the MAXMIND web site, I included the statement as required when importing the 3rd Party Library as shown below.

```
# 3rd Party Libraries
import pygeoip          # 3rd Party Geo IP Lookup
                        # to install geoipy from the command line: pip install pygeoip
                        # This product includes GeoLite data created by MaxMind, available from
                        # <a href="http://www.maxmind.com">http://www.maxmind.com</a>
```

Now that the pygeoip library and associated database geo.dat are installed, I can use them to associate an IP Address with a country. I created a simple function to call and return the country name. If no country can be associated with the given IP address a blank string is returned.

```
#
# Country Lookup
#

def GetCountry(ipAddr):

    # geo.dat download from http://dev.maxmind.com/geoip/legacy/geolite/

    gi = pygeoip.GeoIP('geo.dat')
    return gi.country_name_by_addr(ipAddr)

# End GetCountry Function
```

As with the Host Lookup Method, I provide a toggle that will either set the COUNTRY_LOOKUP variable to True or False depending upon the current state. This is accomplished by the user specifying 'C' option as shown here:

```
elif menuSelection == 'C':

    if COUNTRY_LOOKUP:

        COUNTRY_LOOKUP = False

    else:

        COUNTRY_LOOKUP = True
```

Then anywhere in the code where inclusion of the Country Name would be appropriate the COUNTRY_LOOKUP variable is interrogated and used accordingly.

```
# if Country Lookup is selected

# perform the lookup, else set Country to blank


 if COUNTRY_LOOKUP:

     countryName = GetCountry(serverIP)

 else:

     countryName = ""
```

PERFORMING ANALYSIS

Now that the perfunctory setup is complete, we can execute the individual analysis operations. They include:

1. Printing all observations contained within the loaded observation file
2. Printing the Observed Server List
3. Printing the Observed Client List
4. Printing the Observed Server to Client Connections
5. Printing the Histogram of Observations

Printing Observations All

The printing out of all the Observations simply requires extracting each dictionary entry and printing out the contents. This includes the Server IP Address, Client IP Address, Server Port Number, Port Type (TCP or UDP) along with the number of observations of this unique combination occurring during each hourly period. The method to perform this operation is shown below.

```
# Print the Contents of the Dictionary

def PrintOb(self):
    print >> OUT, "\nIP Observations"
    print >> OUT, "Unique Combinations:    ", str(len(self.Dictionary))
    print >> OUT

    # print Heading

    print >> OUT, '                                                ',
    print >> OUT,"|---------------------------------------- Hourly Observations   --------
----------------------------------------|"
    print >> OUT,'%16s' % "Server",
    print >> OUT,'%16s' % "Client",
    print >> OUT,'%7s'  % "Port",
    print >> OUT,'%5s'  % "Type",

    for i in range(0, 24):
        print  >> OUT,' ',
        print >> OUT,'%02d' % i,
    print >> OUT

    # Print Contents
    for keys,values in self.Dictionary.items():

        print >> OUT,'%16s' % keys[SERVER],
        print >> OUT,'%16s' % keys[CLIENT],
        print >> OUT,'%7s'  % str(keys[PORT]),
        print >> OUT,'%5s'  % keys[TYPE],

        for i in range(0, 24):
            print >> OUT, '%4s' % str(values[i]),
        print >> OUT
```

Executing this code produces the following (abbreviated) result

IP Observations
Unique Combinations: 3358

Server	Client	Port	Type		Hourly Observations																							
				00	01	02	03	04	05	06	07	08	09	10	11	12	13	14	15	16	17	18	19	20	21	22	23
107.22.247.75	192.168.0.10	80	TCP	0	0	0	0	0	0	0	0	0	0	0	0	0	0	0	0	0	0	0	0	0	0	0	23
63.245.217.162	192.168.0.19	443	TCP	0	0	0	0	0	0	0	0	0	0	0	0	0	0	0	106	0	0	0	0	0	0	0	0
64.34.191.25	192.168.0.10	80	TCP	0	0	0	0	0	0	0	0	0	0	0	0	0	0	0	27	0	0	0	0	0	11	0	0
54.236.165.101	192.168.0.10	80	TCP	0	0	0	0	0	0	0	0	0	0	0	0	27	0	0	0	0	0	0	0	0	0	0	0
::																											
:: Abbreviated																											
::																											
54.85.196.104	192.168.0.10	80	TCP	0	0	0	64	21	0	0	0	0	0	0	0	0	0	0	0	0	10	0	0	0	0	0	0
192.168.0.8	192.168.0.1	3893	TCP	0	0	0	0	0	10	0	10	0	0	0	0	0	0	0	0	0	0	0	0	0	0	12	0
192.168.0.8	192.168.0.1	4431	TCP	0	0	0	0	0	0	12	0	0	0	0	0	0	0	0	0	0	0	0	0	0	0	0	0

====== P2NMAP Analysis Menu ======

Printing the Observed Servers

The next analysis function will iterate through the dictionary and provide a sorted list of observed servers. For each server a list of observed service ports supported by the server are also listed. In addition, details such as geolocation (i.e. country), host name and port description will be included based upon the settings specified by the user. The method developed to extract these details from the observations dictionary is shown below.

```
#
# PrintUniqueServer List
#
# Method to Print to Standard Out each Server IP
# Options include: lookupHost and lookupCountry
# If selected, they will perform the respective lookups
# and report data received
#
def PrintServers(self):

    print >> OUT, "\nUnique Server List\n"
    print >> OUT, '-------------------------------------------------------------------------

    # Create "set" of server IP addresses
    # from the Dictionary

    self.servers = set()
    for keys,values in self.Dictionary.items():
        self.servers.add(keys[SERVER])

    # Convert Set to List and Sort
    # This method will ensure unique sorted list

    serverList = list(self.servers)
    serverList.sort()

    # Process Each Server IP in the sorted list

    for serverIP in serverList:

        # if Country Lookup is selected
        # perform the lookup, else set Country to blank
        if COUNTRY_LOOKUP:
            countryName = GetCountry(serverIP)
        else:
            countryName = ""

        # Set a Try / Except Loop in case of network error.

        try:
            # if caller requested hostname lookup
            # perform the lookup, else set name to blank
            if HOST_LOOKUP:
                hostName = socket.gethostbyaddr(serverIP)
            else:
                hostName = ["", "", ""]
        except:
            hostName = ""
            pass

        # Print out formatted results
        print >> OUT,' %15s ' % serverIP,
        print >> OUT,' %15s ' % countryName,
        print >> OUT,' %60s ' % hostName[HOST_NAME]

        self.ports = set()
```

```
            for keys,values in self.Dictionary.items():
                if keys[SERVER] == serverIP:
                    self.ports.add( (keys[PORT], keys[TYPE]) )

        portList = list(self.ports)
        portList.sort()

        for port in portList:
            print >> OUT,' %27s ' % str(port[0]),
            print >> OUT,' %5s ' % port[1],
            print >> OUT,'%40s'  % self.portOB.Lookup(port[0],port[1])
        print >> OUT, '-----------------------------------------------------------------
----'

    print >> OUT, "\n\n"

  # End PrintUniqueServer List
```

Executing this code produces the following (abbreviated) result

```
Unique Server List

--------------------------------------------------------------------------
         0.0.0.0
                            68    UDP              Bootstrap Protocol Client
--------------------------------------------------------------------------
     103.31.6.36           Australia
                            80    TCP                  World Wide Web HTTP
--------------------------------------------------------------------------
  104.130.251.189          United States
                            80    TCP                  World Wide Web HTTP
--------------------------------------------------------------------------
   104.130.53.116          United States
                            80    TCP                  World Wide Web HTTP
...
... Abbreviated
...
--------------------------------------------------------------------------
     192.168.0.1
                            67    UDP              Bootstrap Protocol Server
                          1027    UDP                               Unknown
                          1900    UDP                             UPnP SSDP
--------------------------------------------------------------------------
    192.168.0.10
                            68    UDP              Bootstrap Protocol Client
                           137    UDP                  NETBIOS Name Service
                          5353    UDP                               Unknown
                          8612    UDP                               Unknown
                         17500    UDP                               Unknown
--------------------------------------------------------------------------
   192.168.0.100
                         29808    UDP                               Unknown
--------------------------------------------------------------------------
    192.168.0.11
                          5353    UDP                               Unknown
--------------------------------------------------------------------------
    192.168.0.12
                            68    UDP              Bootstrap Protocol Client
                           137    UDP                  NETBIOS Name Service
                           161    UDP                                  SNMP
                           427    UDP                       Server Location
                          3910    TCP                               Unknown
                          8612    UDP                               Unknown
                          9100    TCP                         HP JetDirect
                         43041    UDP                               Unknown
                         43528    UDP                               Unknown
--------------------------------------------------------------------------
    192.168.0.13
                          5353    UDP                               Unknown
--------------------------------------------------------------------------
```

```
-----------------------------------------------------------------------
    192.168.0.14
                      68       UDP                Bootstrap Protocol Client
                      5353     UDP                                  Unknown
-----------------------------------------------------------------------
    192.168.0.15
                      8612     UDP                                  Unknown
-----------------------------------------------------------------------
    192.168.0.19
                      68       UDP                Bootstrap Protocol Client
                      123      UDP                     Network Time Protocol
                      137      UDP                       NETBIOS Name Service
                      138      UDP                   NETBIOS Datagram Service
                      5353     UDP                                  Unknown
                      8612     UDP                                  Unknown
                      16403    UDP                                  Unknown
                      17500    UDP                                  Unknown
-----------------------------------------------------------------------
    192.168.0.255
                      137      UDP                       NETBIOS Name Service
                      1947     UDP                                 hlserver
                      8612     UDP                                  Unknown
-----------------------------------------------------------------------
```

Printing the Observed Clients

Extracting and printing the list of observed clients is accomplished in the same
manner as that of the observed servers. Once again the output will include details such as geolocation (i.e. country) and host name if they are specified to be
included by the user. The method developed to extract these details from the
observations dictionary is shown below. One question you might ask is why is
the client port not specified?

> Why is the client port not included? Eliminating the client port (which would typically be an
> ephemeral port, and not useful to us) significantly reduces the size of our dictionary. If we
> were to include the ephemeral ports in the dictionary key, virtually every server client con-
> nection would be unique.

```
#
# Print Unique Client List
#
# Method to Print each Client IP.
# Options include: lookupHost and lookupCountry
# If selected, they will perform the respective lookups
# and report data received

def PrintClients(self):

    print >> OUT,"\nUnique Client List\n"

    self.clients = set()
    for keys,values in self.Dictionary.items():
        self.clients.add(keys[1])

    clientList = list(self.clients)
    clientList.sort()

    # Process Each Server IP in the sorted list
```

```
for clientIP in clientList:

    # if Country Lookup is selected
    # perform the lookup, else set Country to blank

        if COUNTRY_LOOKUP:
            countryName = GetCountry(clientIP)
        else:
            countryName = ""

    # Set a Try / Except Loop in case of network error.

        try:
            # if caller requested hostname lookup
            # perform the lookup, else set name to blank
            if HOST_LOOKUP:
                hostName = socket.gethostbyaddr(clientIP)
            else:
                hostName = ["","",""]
        except:
            hostName = ["","",""]
            pass

    # Print out formatted results

        print >> OUT,' %15s ' % clientIP,
        print >> OUT,' %15s ' % countryName,
        print >> OUT,' %60s ' % hostName[HOST_NAME]

    # End PrintUniqueClient List
```

Executing this method produces the following (abbreviated) result:

```
Unique Client List

    118.98.104.21         Indonesia         21.subnet118-98-104.astinet.telkom.net.id
      127.0.0.1                                              Lenovo-UpStairs
  141.212.122.34       United States          researchscan289.eecs.umich.edu
  141.212.122.39       United States          researchscan294.eecs.umich.edu
    169.229.3.91       United States          researchscan1.EECS.Berkeley.EDU

... Abbreviated
...
    37.247.36.119        Netherlands
    41.218.92.89           Namibia          westair-schneider-int.cust.na.afrisp.net
     46.4.7.155            Germany                        plesksolutions.com
    50.17.79.135       United States     ec2-50-17-79-135.compute-1.amazonaws.com

========== P2NMAP Analysis Menu ==========
```

Printing the Observed Server to Client Connections

Another interesting way to view the results of the observation, is to list each
server and include all client connections made to that server. This provides the

comprehensive server / client connection list. This method is slightly more complex, since the dictionary must first generate the list of observed servers, and then generate a list of clients that connected over any port to that server. The method developed to extract these details from the observations dictionary is shown below.

```
#
# Print Detailed Server List
#
# Method to Print to Standard Out
# Unique Server / Client Interactions
#

def PrintServerDetails(self):

    # Create "set" of server IP addresses
    # from the Dictionary

    self.servers = set()

    for keys,values in self.Dictionary.items():
        self.servers.add(keys[SERVER])
        # Convert Set to List and Sort
        # This method will ensure unique sorted list

    # Now create a sorted list of unique servers
    serverList = list(self.servers)
    serverList.sort()

    # Now Iterate through the server list
    # finding all the matching server connections
    # and provide connection details

    for serverIP in serverList:

        # if Country Lookup is selected
        # perform the lookup, else set Country to blank
        if COUNTRY_LOOKUP:
            countryName = GetCountry(serverIP)
        else:
            countryName = ""

        # Set a Try / Except Loop in case of network error.

        try:
            # if caller requested hostname lookup
            # perform the lookup, else set name to blank
            if HOST_LOOKUP:
                hostName = socket.gethostbyaddr(serverIP)
            else:
                hostName = ["", "", ""]
        except:
            hostName = ""
            continue
```

```
# Print out formatted results
print >> OUT,"\n==========================================================="
print >> OUT,"Server: ",
print >> OUT,' %15s ' % serverIP,
print >> OUT,' %15s ' % countryName,
print >> OUT,' %60s ' % hostName[HOST_NAME]
print >> OUT,"==========================================================="
print >> OUT,'%16s' % "Client",
print >> OUT,'%7s'  % "Port",
print >> OUT,'%40s'  % "Port Description",
print >> OUT,'%5s'   % "Type",
print >> OUT

for keys,values in self.Dictionary.items():

    # If server matches current
    # print out the details:

    if keys[SERVER] == serverIP:
        print >> OUT,'%16s' % keys[CLIENT],
        print >> OUT,'%7s'  % str(keys[PORT]),
        print >> OUT,'%40s'  % self.portOB.Lookup(keys[PORT],keys[TYPE]),
        print >> OUT,'%5s'  % keys[TYPE]

# End PrintUniqueServer List
```

Executing this method produces the following (abbreviated) result:

```
Unique Server Client Connection List
---------------------------------------------------------------------------

===========================================================
Server:        0.0.0.0
===========================================================
         Client   Port                        Port Description  Type
  255.255.255.255    68         Bootstrap Protocol Client   UDP

===========================================================
Server:     103.31.6.36       Australia
===========================================================
         Client   Port                        Port Description  Type
   192.168.0.10     80          World Wide Web HTTP   TCP

===========================================================
Server:   104.130.251.189     United States
===========================================================
         Client   Port                        Port Description  Type
   192.168.0.10     80          World Wide Web HTTP   TCP

===========================================================
Server:   104.130.53.116      United States
===========================================================
         Client   Port                        Port Description  Type
   192.168.0.10     80          World Wide Web HTTP   TCP
...
... Abbreviated Output
...
===========================================================
Server:     96.6.113.90       United States
```

```
=============================================================
          Client    Port                   Port Description  Type
    192.168.0.10      80                    World Wide Web HTTP  TCP

=============================================================
Server:    98.137.170.33     United States
=============================================================
          Client    Port                   Port Description  Type
    192.168.0.10      80                    World Wide Web HTTP  TCP

=============================================================
Server:    98.139.225.168    United States
=============================================================
          Client    Port                   Port Description  Type
    192.168.0.10     443           HTTP protocol over TLS/SSL  TCP
    192.168.0.10      80                    World Wide Web HTTP  TCP

=============================================================
Server:    98.139.225.35     United States
=============================================================
          Client    Port                   Port Description  Type
    192.168.0.15      80                    World Wide Web HTTP  TCP
```

Printing a Histogram of Observations

The final extraction will add to the detailed server / client connection list and
provide a histogram of activities for each server and client interaction. The
Histogram produced is for a 24 hour time table. If the P2NMAP-Capture script
is run for multiple days the activities for each hour will be cumulative. This
allows the investigator to quickly observe activities occurring at unusual times
of the day, activities that occur only a small number of times, or possibly only
once. This can potentially indicate a heartbeat or beacon generated by a malicious application. The method developed to extract these details from the
observations dictionary is shown below.

```python
#
# Print Capture Histogram
#
# Method to Print a
# Histogram for each Entry
#

def PrintHistogram(self):

    # Create "set" of server IP addresses
    # from the Dictionary

    print >> OUT,"\nHourly Histogram\n"

    self.servers = set()

    for keys,values in self.Dictionary.items():
        self.servers.add(keys[SERVER])
        # Convert Set to List and Sort
        # This method will ensure unique sorted list
```

```
    # Now create a sorted list of unique servers
    serverList = list(self.servers)
    serverList.sort()

    # Now Iterate through the server list
    # finding all the matching server connections

# and provide connection details

for serverIP in serverList:

    # if Country Lookup is selected
    # perform the lookup, else set Country to blank

    if COUNTRY_LOOKUP:
        countryName = GetCountry(serverIP)
    else:
        countryName = ""

    # Set a Try / Except Loop in case of network error.

    try:
        # if caller requested hostname lookup
        # perform the lookup, else set name to blank
        if HOST_LOOKUP:
            hostName = socket.gethostbyaddr(serverIP)
        else:
            hostName = ["", "", ""]
    except:
        hostName = ["", "", ""]
        continue

    # Print out formatted results
    print >> OUT,"\n==========================================================="
    print >> OUT,"Server: ",
    print >> OUT,' %15s ' % serverIP,
    print >> OUT,' %15s ' % countryName,
    print >> OUT,' %60s ' % hostName[HOST_NAME]
    print >> OUT,"==========================================================="

    for keys,values in self.Dictionary.items():

        # If server matches current
        # print out the histogram

        if keys[SERVER] == serverIP:
            if keys[SERVER] == serverIP:
                print >> OUT,'%16s' % "Client",
                print >> OUT,'%7s'  % "Port",
                print >> OUT,'%40s' % "Port Description",
                print >> OUT,'%5s'  % "Type",
                print >> OUT
                print >> OUT,'%16s' % keys[CLIENT],
                print >> OUT,'%7s'  % str(keys[PORT]),
                print >> OUT,'%40s' % self.portOB.Lookup(keys[PORT],keys[TYPE]),
                print >> OUT,'%5s'  % keys[TYPE]
                print >> OUT
                print >> OUT,"HR "
                self.Histogram(values)

# End Histogram Output
```

Executing this method produces the following (abbreviated) result

```
Hourly Histogram
=============================================================
Server:              0.0.0.0
=============================================================
        Client      Port                        Port Description    Type
   255.255.255.255    68               Bootstrap Protocol Client    UDP

HR
00: * (3)
01: * (2)
02: * (3)
03: * (2)
04: * (2)
05: * (3)
06: * (2)
07: * (2)
08: * (1)
09: ****************************************************************************** (518)
10: *********** (65)
11: * (5)
12: * (2)
13: * (8)
14: ** (12)
15: * (2)
16: * (2)
17: ** (11)
18: * (2)
19: * (2)
20: * (2)
21: * (3)
22: * (2)
23: * (5)



=============================================================
Server:     103.31.6.36       Australia
=============================================================
        Client    Port                          Port Description    Type
   192.168.0.10    80                    World Wide Web HTTP    TCP

HR
00:
01:
02:
03:
04:
05:
06:
07:
08:
09:
10:
11:
12:
13:
14: *********************************************************************************** (39)
15:
16:
17:
18:
19:
20:
21:
22:
23:



=============================================================
Server:   104.130.251.189    United States
=============================================================
        Client    Port                          Port Description    Type
   192.168.0.10    80                    World Wide Web HTTP    TCP

HR
00:
01:
02:
03:
04:
05:
06:
07:
08:
09:
10:
11:
12:
13:
14:
15: *********************************************************************************** (17)
16:
17:
```

```
18:
19:
20:
21:
22:
23:
… Abbreviated
…
==================================================
Server:    23.218.114.120    United States
==================================================
         Client    Port                  Port Description  Type
     192.168.0.10    80               World Wide Web HTTP   TCP

HR
00:
01:
02:
03:
04: ******************************* (16)
05: ******************************** (17)
06: ****************************** (15)
07: ******************************** (17)
08: ********************************** (19)
09:
10: ************************************************** (28)
11: ********************************************** (24)
12:
13: ********************************************************************************* (44)
14: ********************************************************** (32)
15: ****************************** (15)
16: ***************************** (14)
17: ***************************** (14)
18: ********************************************** (24)
19: ***************************************************** (30)
20: ************************************************ (21)
21: ****************************** (19)
22:
23: ******************************** (17)


==================================================
Server:    23.218.114.211    United States
==================================================
         Client    Port                  Port Description  Type
     192.168.0.10   443           HTTP protocol over TLS/SSL  TCP

HR
C0:
C1:
C2:
C3:
C4: ****************************************************************************** (66)
C5: ********************************************************** (39)
C6: ************************************************************ (42)
C7:
C8:
C9:
10:
11:
12:
13:
14:
15:
16:
17:
18:
19:
20:
21: ********************************************************************************* (70)
22:
23:


==================================================
Server:    23.218.121.55    United States
==================================================
         Client    Port                  Port Description  Type
     192.168.0.10    80               World Wide Web HTTP   TCP

HR
C0:
C1:
C2:
C3: ******************************************************** (107)
C4: ********************************** (68)
C5:
C6:
C7:
C8:
C9:
```

```
10:
11:
12:
13:
14:
15: ******************************** (66)
16:
17:
18:
19:
20:
21: ******************************************************************************** (192)
22:
23:
```

Final P2NMAP-Anaysis.py Script Complete Source Code

The final P2NMAP-Analysis.py script is shown here. Note that the entire script is a single Python file and requires no arguments to execute. However, there are a couple of assumptions.

1. The "geo.dat" file must be included in the source directory
2. The pygeoip 3rd Party Library has been installed using:

   $ **pip install pygeoip**

   or

   C:\> **pip install pygeoip**

3. You have a populated IP dictionary file that was generated by the P2NMAP-Capture script.

```python
#
# P2NMA-Analyze.py Script
#
# Perform analysis of previously capture .ipdict files
#

import argparse        # Python Standard Library - Parser for command-line options, arguments
import os              # operating system functions i.e. file I/O
import datetime        # Python Standard Library date and time methods
import pickle          # Python Standard Library pickle methods
import socket          # Python Standard Library Low Level Networking
import sys             # Python Standard Library Low Level System Methods

# 3rd Party Libraries
import pygeoip         # 3rd Party Geo IP Lookup
                       # pip install pygeoip
                       # This product includes GeoLite data created by MaxMind, available from
                       # <a href="http://www.maxmind.com">http://www.maxmind.com</a>.

# import matplotlib.pyplot as plt  # Import 3rd Party Plotting Library

# DEFINE PSUEDO CONSTANTS

SERVER    = 0  # Server key index
CLIENT    = 1  # Client key index
PORT      = 2  # Port    key index
TYPE      = 3  # Type    key index ("TCP" or "UDP")
HOST_NAME = 0  # HOST NAME index return from gethostbyaddr

# Note these are set by menu selection
```

```
HOST_LOOKUP      = False   # gethostbyaddr() will obtain Host Name
COUNTRY_LOOKUP = False   # Country Name wil be associated with IP
PRINT_STDOUT    = True    # If True, all output and menu selections directed
                         # If False, all output directed to a file except menu

OUT              = sys.stdout       # Default Output to Standard Out

OSOB_LOADED     = False             # OS Observations Loaded Flag

#
# Country Lookup
#

def GetCountry(ipAddr):

    # download from http://dev.maxmind.com/geoip/legacy/geolite/
    gi = pygeoip.GeoIP('geo.dat')
    return gi.country_name_by_addr(ipAddr)

# End GetCountry Function

#
# Name: ValFileRead
#
# Desc: Function that will validate a file exists and is readable
#       Used for argument validation only
#
# Input: a file Path
#
# Actions:
#              if valid will return a full file path
#
#              if invalid it will raise an ArgumentTypeError within argparse
#              which will inturn be reported by argparse to the user
#

def ValFileRead(theFile):

    # Validate the path is a File
    if not os.path.exists(theFile):
        raise argparse.ArgumentTypeError('File does not exist')

    # Validate the path is Readable
    if os.access(theFile, os.R_OK):
        return theFile
    else:
        raise argparse.ArgumentTypeError('File is not readable')

#End ValFileRead ======================================

#
# Port Lookup Class
#
class PortsClass:

    # Constructor

    def __init__(self, portTextFile):
```

```python
#Attributes of the Object
self.portDictionary = {}

# Open the PortList Text File
with open(portTextFile, 'r') as infile:

    # Process EachLine
    for nextLine in infile:

        lineList = nextLine.split()
        # Make sure we have a valid input line

        if len(lineList) >= 3:
            # Split the line into parts

            # lineList[0] == PortType   (TCP or UDP)
            # lineList[1] == PortNumber

                    # Determine how many parts we have after type and port

                    #portDescList = lineList[2:]
                    portDesc = ' '.join(lineList[2:])

                    # Now create a dictionary entry
                    # key = Port,Type

                    # Value = Description

                    self.portDictionary[(lineList[1], lineList[0])] = portDesc
            else:
                    # Skip this line
                    continue

    def Lookup(self, portNumber, portType):

        try:
            portDesc = self.portDictionary[str(portNumber),portType]
        except:
            portDesc = "Unknown"

        return portDesc

# End PortsClass Definition


#
# Class: IPObservationDictionary
#
# Desc: Handles all methods and properties
#       relating to the IPOservations
#
#

class IPObservationDictionary:

    # Constructor

    def __init__(self):
```

```
    #Attributes of the Object

    # Dictionary to Hold IP Observations
    self.Dictionary = {}
    self.observationsLoaded  = False
    self.observationFileName = ""

    # Instantiate the PortsClass Object
    # Creates and object that can be used
    # to lookup port descriptions
    #

    self.portOB = PortsClass("PortList.txt")

# Method to Add an observation

def AddOb(self, key):

    # Obtain the current hour

    now = datetime.datetime.now()
    hour = now.hour

    # Check to see if key is already in the dictionary

    if key in self.Dictionary:

        # If yes, retrieve the current value
        curValue = self.Dictionary[key]

        # Increment the count for the current hour
        curValue[hour-1] = curValue[hour-1] + 1

        # Update the value associated with this key
        self.Dictionary[key] = curValue

    else:
        # if the key doesn't yet exist
        # Create one

        curValue = [0,0,0,0,0,0,0,0,0,0,0,0,0,0,0,0,0,0,0,0,0,0,0,0]

        # Increment the count for the current hour
        curValue[hour-1] = curValue[hour-1] + 1

        self.Dictionary[key] = curValue

# Method to retrieve an observation
# If no observation found return None

def GetOb(self,key):

    if key in self.Dictionary:
        curValue = self.Dictionary[key]
        return curValue
    else:
        return None

# Print the Contents of the Dictionary
```

```
def PrintOb(self):
    print >> OUT, "\nIP Observations"
    print >> OUT, "Unique Combinations:     ", str(len(self.Dictionary))
    print >> OUT

    # print Heading

    print >> OUT, '                                                      ',
    print >> OUT,"|---------------------------------------- Hourly Observations  --------
----------------------------------------|"
        print >> OUT,'%16s' % "Server",
        print >> OUT,'%16s' % "Client",
        print >> OUT,'%7s'  % "Port",
        print >> OUT,'%5s'  % "Type"
        print >> OUT,'----------------------------------------------------------------------
-------------------------------------------------------------------------------'
        print >> OUT,'                                                      ',
        for i in range(0, 24):
            print  >> OUT,' ',
            print >> OUT,'%02d' % i,
        print >> OUT

        # Print Contents
        for keys,values in self.Dictionary.items():

            print >> OUT,'%16s' % keys[SERVER],
            print >> OUT,'%16s' % keys[CLIENT],
            print >> OUT,'%7s'  % str(keys[PORT]),
            print >> OUT,'%5s'  % keys[TYPE],

            for i in range(0, 24):
                print >> OUT, '%4s' % str(values[i]),

            print >> OUT

    print >> OUT, "\nEnd Print Observations\n"

    def Histogram(self, observations):
        """
        Histogram data to stdout
        """
        largest = max(observations)
        scale = 100. / largest
        for hr, datum in enumerate(observations):
            bar = "*" * int(datum * scale)
            if bar == "" and datum > 0:
                bar = "*"
                print >> OUT, "%02d: %s (%d)" % (hr, bar, datum)
            elif datum != 0:
                print >> OUT, "%02d: %s (%d)" % (hr, bar, datum)
            else:
                print >> OUT, "%02d:" % hr
        print >> OUT, "\n"

    #
    # PrintUniqueServer List
    #
    # Method to Print to Standard Out each Server IP
```

```
# Options include: lookupHost and lookupCountry
# If selected, they will perform the respective lookups
# and report data received
#

def PrintServers(self):

    print >> OUT, "\nUnique Server List\n"
    print >> OUT, '----------------------------------------------------------------------

    # Create "set" of server IP addresses
    # from the Dictionary

    self.servers = set()
    for keys,values in self.Dictionary.items():
        self.servers.add(keys[SERVER])

    # Convert Set to List and Sort
    # This method will ensure unique sorted list

    serverList = list(self.servers)
    serverList.sort()

    # Process Each Server IP in the sorted list

    for serverIP in serverList:

        # if Country Lookup is selected
        # perform the lookup, else set Country to blank
        if COUNTRY_LOOKUP:
            countryName = GetCountry(serverIP)
        else:
            countryName = ""

        # Set a Try / Except Loop in case of network error.

        try:
            # if caller requested hostname lookup
            # perform the lookup, else set name to blank
            if HOST_LOOKUP:
                hostName = socket.gethostbyaddr(serverIP)
            else:
                hostName = ["", "", ""]
        except:
            hostName = ""
            pass

        # Print out formatted results
        print >> OUT,' %15s ' % serverIP,
        print >> OUT,' %15s ' % countryName,
        print >> OUT,' %60s ' % hostName[HOST_NAME]

        self.ports = set()

        for keys,values in self.Dictionary.items():
            if keys[SERVER] == serverIP:
                self.ports.add( (keys[PORT], keys[TYPE]) )
```

```
            portList = list(self.ports)
            portList.sort()

            for port in portList:
                print >> OUT,' %27s ' % str(port[0]),
                print >> OUT,' %5s ' % port[1],
                print >> OUT,'%40s'  % self.portOB.Lookup(port[0],port[1])
            print >> OUT, '-----------------------------------------------------------------------
----'

        print >> OUT
        print >> OUT, "End Print Servers\n"
        print >> OUT, "\n\n"

    # End PrintUniqueServer List


    #
    # Print Detailed Server List
    #
    # Method to Print to Standard Out
    # Unique Server / Client Interactions
    #

    def PrintServerDetails(self):

        # Create "set" of server IP addresses
        # from the Dictionary
        print >> OUT, "\nUnique Server Client Connection List\n"
        print >> OUT, '-----------------------------------------------------------------------


        self.servers = set()

        for keys,values in self.Dictionary.items():
            self.servers.add(keys[SERVER])
            # Convert Set to List and Sort
            # This method will ensure unique sorted list

        # Now create a sorted list of unique servers
        serverList = list(self.servers)
        serverList.sort()

        # Now Iterate through the server list
        # finding all the matching server connections
        # and provide connection details

        for serverIP in serverList:

            # if Country Lookup is selected
            # perform the lookup, else set Country to blank
            if COUNTRY_LOOKUP:
                countryName = GetCountry(serverIP)
            else:
                countryName = ""

            # Set a Try / Except Loop in case of network error.
            try:
```

```
            # if caller requested hostname lookup
            # perform the lookup, else set name to blank
            if HOST_LOOKUP:
                hostName = socket.gethostbyaddr(serverIP)
            else:
                hostName = ["", "", ""]
        except:
            hostName = ""
            continue

        # Print out formatted results
        print >> OUT,"\n==========================================================="
        print >> OUT,"Server: ",
        print >> OUT,' %15s ' % serverIP,
        print >> OUT,' %15s ' % countryName,
        print >> OUT,' %60s ' % hostName[HOST_NAME]
        print >> OUT,"==========================================================="
        print >> OUT,'%16s' % "Client",
        print >> OUT,'%7s'  % "Port",
        print >> OUT,'%40s'  % "Port Description",
        print >> OUT,'%5s'   % "Type",
        print >> OUT

        for keys,values in self.Dictionary.items():

            # If server matches current
            # print out the details:

            if keys[SERVER] == serverIP:
                print >> OUT,'%16s' % keys[CLIENT],
                print >> OUT,'%7s'  % str(keys[PORT]),
                print >> OUT,'%40s'  % self.portOB.Lookup(keys[PORT],keys[TYPE]),
                print >> OUT,'%5s'  % keys[TYPE]
    print >> OUT
    print >> OUT, "End Print Server Details\n"

# End PrintUniqueServer List

#
# Print Capture Histogram
#
# Method to Print a
# Histogram for each Entry
#

def PrintHistogram(self):

    # Create "set" of server IP addresses
    # from the Dictionary

    print >> OUT,"\nHourly Histogram\n"

    self.servers = set()

    for keys,values in self.Dictionary.items():
        self.servers.add(keys[SERVER])
        # Convert Set to List and Sort
        # This method will ensure unique sorted list
```

```
# Now create a sorted list of unique servers
serverList = list(self.servers)
serverList.sort()

# Now Iterate through the server list
# finding all the matching server connections
# and provide connection details

for serverIP in serverList:

    # if Country Lookup is selected
    # perform the lookup, else set Country to blank

    if COUNTRY_LOOKUP:
        countryName = GetCountry(serverIP)
    else:
        countryName = ""

    # Set a Try / Except Loop in case of network error.

    try:
        # if caller requested hostname lookup
        # perform the lookup, else set name to blank
        if HOST_LOOKUP:
            hostName = socket.gethostbyaddr(serverIP)
        else:
            hostName = ["", "", ""]
    except:
            hostName = ["", "", ""]
            continue

        # Print out formatted results
        print >> OUT,"\n============================================================="
        print >> OUT,"Server: ",
        print >> OUT,' %15s ' % serverIP,
        print >> OUT,' %15s ' % countryName,
        print >> OUT,' %60s ' % hostName[HOST_NAME]
        print >> OUT,"============================================================="

        for keys,values in self.Dictionary.items():

            # If server matches current
            # print out the histogram

            if keys[SERVER] == serverIP:
                if keys[SERVER] == serverIP:
                    print >> OUT,'%16s' % "Client",
                    print >> OUT,'%7s'  % "Port",
                    print >> OUT,'%40s' % "Port Description",
                    print >> OUT,'%5s'  % "Type",
                    print >> OUT
                    print >> OUT,'%16s' % keys[CLIENT],
                    print >> OUT,'%7s'  % str(keys[PORT]),
                    print >> OUT,'%40s' % self.portOB.Lookup(keys[PORT],keys[TYPE]),
                    print >> OUT,'%5s'  % keys[TYPE]
                    print >> OUT
                    print >> OUT,"HR "
                    self.Histogram(values)
```

```
        print >> OUT
        print >> OUT, "End Print Histogram\n"

# End Histogram Output


    #
    # Print Unique Client List
    #
    # Method to Print Out each Client IP
    # Options include: lookupHost and lookupCountry
    # If selected, they will perform the respective lookups
    # and report data received

    def PrintClients(self):

        print >> OUT,"\nUnique Client List\n"

        self.clients = set()
        for keys,values in self.Dictionary.items():
            self.clients.add(keys[1])

        clientList = list(self.clients)
        clientList.sort()

        # Process Each Server IP in the sorted list

        for clientIP in clientList:

            # if Country Lookup is selected
            # perform the lookup, else set Country to blank
            if COUNTRY_LOOKUP:
                countryName = GetCountry(clientIP)
            else:
                countryName = ""

            # Set a Try / Except Loop in case of network error.

            try:
                # if caller requested hostname lookup
                # perform the lookup, else set name to blank
                if HOST_LOOKUP:
                    hostName = socket.gethostbyaddr(clientIP)
                else:
                    hostName = ["","",""]
            except:
                hostName = ["","",""]
                pass

            # Print out formatted results

            print >> OUT,' %15s ' % clientIP,
            print >> OUT,' %15s ' % countryName,
            print >> OUT,' %60s ' % hostName[HOST_NAME]

        print >> OUT, "\nEnd Print Client List\n"
```

```
        # End PrintUniqueClient List


    # Save the Current Observation Dictionary
    # to the specified file

    def SaveOb(self, fileName):

        with open(fileName, 'wb') as fp:
            pickle.dump(self.Dictionary, fp)

    # Load in and Observation Dictionary
    # from the specified file

    def LoadOb(self, fileName):
        try:
            with open(fileName, 'rb') as fp:
                self.Dictionary = pickle.loads(fp.read())
                self.observationFileName = fileName
                self.observationsLoaded  = True
        except:
            print "Loading Observations - Failed"
            self.observationsLoaded  = False
            self.observationFileName = fileName

    def PrintIPAnalysisMenu(self):

        print "========== P2NMAP Analysis Menu ==========\n"

        if self.observationsLoaded:
            print "Current Observation File: ", self.observationFileName
            print

        print "[L]    Load Observation File for Analysis"

    if self.observationsLoaded:
        if PRINT_STDOUT:
            print "[O]    Direct Output to File   (Current = Stdout)"
        else:
            print "[O]    Direct Output to Stdout (Current = results.txt)"

        if HOST_LOOKUP:
            print "[H]    Turn Off Host Lookup    (Current = Host Lookup On)"
        else:
            print "[H]    Turn On Host Lookup     (Current = Host Lookup Off)"

        if COUNTRY_LOOKUP:
            print "[C]    Turn Off Country Lookup (Current = Country Lookup On)"
        else:
            print "[C]    Turn On Country Lookup  (Current = Country Lookup Off)"

        print "=============================================================="
        print "[1]    Print Observations      (ALL)"
        print "[2]    Print Servers           (Unique)"
        print "[3]    Print Clients           (Unique)"
        print "[4]    Print Connections       (Unique by Server)"
        print "[5]    Print Histogram"
        print
print "[X]    Exit P2NMAP Analysis"
```

```
        print

    # Destructor Delete the Object

    def __del__(self):
        if VERBOSE:
            print >> OUT,"Closed"

# End IPObservationClass =====================================


# Main Program Starts Here
#===================================

if __name__ == '__main__':

    # Set VERBOSE to True
    VERBOSE = True

    # Create an ip observation object

    ipOB = IPObservationDictionary()

    while True:

        ipOB.PrintIPAnalysisMenu()

        menuSelection = raw_input("Enter Selection: ").upper()
        if menuSelection == 'L':
            fileName = raw_input("Enter IP Capture File: ")
            ipOB.LoadOb(fileName)
            print

        elif menuSelection == 'O':
            if PRINT_STDOUT:
                PRINT_STDOUT = False
                OUT = open("results.txt", 'w+')
            else:
                PRINT_STDOUT = True
                OUT.close()
                OUT = sys.stdout
        elif menuSelection == 'H':
            if HOST_LOOKUP:
                HOST_LOOKUP = False
            else:
                HOST_LOOKUP = True

        elif menuSelection == 'C':
            if COUNTRY_LOOKUP:
                COUNTRY_LOOKUP = False
            else:
                COUNTRY_LOOKUP = True
        elif menuSelection == '1':
            ipOB.PrintOb()
        elif menuSelection == '2':
            ipOB.PrintServers()
```

```
            elif menuSelection == '3':
                ipOB.PrintClients()
            elif menuSelection == '4':
                ipOB.PrintServerDetails()
            elif menuSelection == '5':
                ipOB.PrintHistogram()
            elif menuSelection == 'X':
                break
            else:
                print "Entry not recognized"
                continue

            OUT.flush()

    print >> OUT, "End P2NMAP"
```

Now you are ready to execute P2NMAP-Analysis.py

$ python P2NMAP-Analysis.py

or

C:\> python P2NMAP-Analysis.py

This will yield the following menu selections and you can start experimenting with the differing modes of operation and analysis functions.

```
========== P2NMAP Analysis Menu ==========

[L]    Load Observation File for Analysis
[X]    Exit P2NMAP Analysis

Enter Selection: l
Enter IP Capture File: test.ipDict

========== P2NMAP Analysis Menu ==========

Current Observation File:  test.ipDict

[L]    Load Observation File for Analysis
[O]    Direct Output to File   (Current = Stdout)
[H]    Turn On Host Lookup     (Current = Host Lookup Off)
[C]    Turn On Country Lookup  (Current = Country Lookup Off)
==============================================================
[1]    Print Observations      (ALL)
[2]    Print Servers           (Unique)
[3]    Print Clients           (Unique)
[4]    Print Connections       (Unique by Server)
[5]    Print Histogram

[X]    Exit P2NMAP Analysis

Enter Selection:
```

REVIEW

In Chapter 4, I leveraged the .ipdict file created in Chapter 3 using the P2NMAP-Capture Script. This file contains the complete dump of the IP observations dictionary. By utilizing this observations dictionary, I created several key methods within the ipObservationsDictionary Class. These methods perform operations including: Printing the complete IP Observations Dictionary, Generating a Comprehensive Server and Client List, Generating a detailed Server / Client Connection List and a detailed histogram of the observation data. In addition, I extrapolated key information from the observed data including Host Name based on the Observation IP Address, Detailed Port Descriptions based on the server ports in use and geographic location of many of the observed servers and clients. Finally, I created a simple menu driven interface that can be used to experiment with the newly created analysis methods.

SUMMARY QUESTIONS

1. What additional analysis methods could be created from the observed data?
2. What filters could be created that would reduce the output and allow the analyst to focus in on targeted data? For example, "Generate a Histogram of any connections that occur less than n times during the observations. Or generate a server / client list for those devices operating outside the U.S.

Additional Resource

Seitz, Justin, 2015. Black Hat Python, Python Programming for Hackers and Pentesters. No Starch Press, San Francisco, California, ISBN: 13-978-1-59327-590-7.

PCAP Extractor and OS Fingerprinting

"It is by doubting that we come to investigate, and by investigating that we recognize the truth."

Peter Abelard

PCAP EXTRACTION

When performing incident response activities, mapping a network or performing penetration testing, you are likely to run in to situations where packet captures have already occurred. This could be in response to an event, or in today's world, more often as a routine practice. Either way, the packet capture (pcap) files can provide valuable information that we can examine and report on using P2NMAP-Analzer.py, which was developed in Chapter 4.

In order to accomplish this, I needed to develop a script that would extract the pertinent data from an existing pcap file and create both an .ipDict and .osDict file that can be processed. In other words, we need to interpret the pcap file to generate the same output files that P2NMAP-Capture.py does.

A number of years ago, Dug Song produced the Python Module dpkt (among many others) that is ideally suited for processing existing packet captures such as pcap files. I have tested the module extensively, and it is a nice addition to your core library within Python. One criticism of the library is the lack of documentation, however our use of the library is pretty straight-forward and my script will hopefully clear up the usage for at least our use case.

Installing dpkt as with most 3rd party Python packages is quite simple: The following command lines work just fine on Windows, Linux and Mac.

Windows:

```
pip install dpkt
```

Linux/Mac:

```
sudo pip install dpkt
```

Whenever I install a new package/module within Python, I run a quick veri-fication that it is working. To do this, I can launch a Python shell from either the Windows or Linux command prompt. Below I show this from a Windows session. I then use the built-in Python import command to load the package. Once the package has been successfully imported you can then use the built-in Python dir() function to print the attributes associated with the package. For even more information you can also use the built-in help() function.

Note, if the import functions fails, it would indicate that the dpkt package is not properly installed.

```
Microsoft Windows [Version 6.3.9600]
(c) 2013 Microsoft Corporation. All rights reserved.

C:\Users\Chet>python
Python 2.7.7 (default, Jun  1 2014, 14:17:13) [MSC v.1500 32 bit (Intel)] on win32
Type "help", "copyright", "credits" or "license" for more information.
>>> import dpkt
>>> dir(dpkt)
['Error', 'NeedData', 'PackError', 'Packet', 'UnpackError', '__author__', '__builtins__',
'__copyright__', '__doc__', '__file__', '__license__', '__name__', '__package__', '__path__'
, '__url__', '__version__', 'ah', 'aim', 'aoe', 'aoeata', 'aoecfg', 'arp', 'array', 'asn1', 'bgp',
'cdp', 'copy', 'crc32c', 'dhcp', 'diameter', 'dns', 'dpkt', 'dtp', 'esp', 'ethernet
', 'gre', 'gzip', 'h225', 'hexdump', 'hsrp', 'http', 'icmp', 'icmp6', 'ieee80211', 'igmp',
'in_cksum', 'in_cksum_add', 'in_cksum_done', 'ip', 'ip6', 'ipx', 'itertools', 'llc', 'loopb
ack', 'mrt', 'netbios', 'netflow', 'ntp', 'ospf', 'pcap', 'pim', 'pmap', 'ppp', 'pppoe', 'qq',
'radiotap', 'radius', 'rfb', 'rip', 'rpc', 'rtp', 'rx', 'sccp', 'sctp', 'sip', 'sll', '
smb', 'socket', 'ssl', 'ssl_ciphersuites', 'stp', 'struct', 'stun', 'tcp', 'telnet', 'tftp',
'tns', 'tpkt', 'udp', 'vrrp', 'yahoo']

>>> help(dpkt)
Help on package dpkt:

NAME
    dpkt - fast, simple packet creation and parsing.

FILE
    c:\python27\lib\site-packages\dpkt\__init__.py

PACKAGE CONTENTS
    ah
    aim
    aoe
    aoeata
    aoecfg
    arp
    asn1
    bgp
    cdp
    crc32c
    dhcp
    diameter
    dns
    dpkt
    dtp
    esp
    ethernet
    gre
    gzip
    h225
```

```
        hsrp
        http
        icmp
        icmp6
        ieee80211
        igmp
        ip
        ip6
        ipx
        llc
        loopback
        mrt
        netbios
        netflow
        ntp
        ospf
        pcap
        pim
        pmap
        ppp
        pppoe
        qq
        radiotap
        radius
        rfb
        rip
        rpc
        rtp
        rx
        sccp
        sctp
        sip
        sll
        smb
        snoop
        ssl
        ssl_ciphersuites
        stp
        stun
        tcp
        telnet
        tftp
        tns
        tpkt
        udp
        vrrp
        yahoo
DATA
        __author__ = 'Dug Song <dugsong@monkey.org>'
        __copyright__ = 'Copyright (c) 2004 Dug Song'
        __license__ = 'BSD'
        __url__ = 'http://dpkt.googlecode.com/'
        __version__ = '1.8.6'
VERSION
        1.8.6

AUTHOR
        Dug Song dugsong@monkey.org
```

Review of P2NMAP-Capture

As you know from the development of the P2NMAP-Capture.py script for network mapping and OS Fingerprinting, we only require a few key pieces of data. We organize that data within an efficient data structure that both minimizes the size and also allows fast processing of the resulting data.

The core data we need from the pcap records in order to properly generate .ipDict and .osDict files are as follows:

General:

- Packet Timestamp
- .ipdict
- Source IP
- Destination IP
- Source Port
- Destination Port
- Protocol (TCP or UDP)
- .osDict
- Source IP
- Destination IP
- Source Port
- Destination Port
- SYN Flag
- DF Flag
- TTL (Time to live value)
- TOS (Type of service value)
- Window Size

Utilizing the dptk Package

The Code to extract the necessary data from the pcap files is isolated here (note: to simplify the code, I left out the exception processing, which is in the full version of the script). Minus the comment line, less than 20 lines of code are required to obtain the fields we require.

```
import dpkt                       # 3rd Party Packet Parsing Module
from dpkt.udp import UDP          # Import specific objects from DPKT for convience
from dpkt.tcp import TCP          #

# Use dpkt and setup a pcapReader Object

pcapReader = dpkt.pcap.Reader(file(inFile, "rb"))

# Using the pcapReader Object process the
# the contents of the selected pcap file

# each interation through the loop will return
# 1) packet timestamp
# 2) packet raw data

for timeStamp, pckData in pcapReader:

    # Next I retrieve the etherNet packet contents
```

```
etherNet = dpkt.ethernet.Ethernet(pckData)

# Verify that this ethernet packet carries an IP Packet

if etherNet.type == dpkt.ethernet.ETH_TYPE_IP:

    # get the ip data and extract the source and destination ip addresses
    # use the socket module to convert them to dot notational form

    # Decode the source and destination IP Address

    ip = etherNet.data
    sourceAddress      = socket.inet_ntoa(ip.src)
    destinationAddress = socket.inet_ntoa(ip.dst)
    # Check Packet Type (either TCP or UDP and process accordingly)

    if type(ip.data) == TCP :

        # Extract and Decode the Ports in use
        tcp = ip.data

        # Obtain Data for OS Fingerprinting

        # SYN Flag
        SYN = ( tcp.flags & dpkt.tcp.TH_SYN ) != 0

        # DF Flag
        DF = ( tcp.flags & dpkt.tcp.TH_URG ) != 0

        # Window Size
        WINDOW_SIZE = tcp.win

        # Time to Live and Type of Service values
        TTL = ip.ttl
        TOS = ip.tos

        # Now obtain the Source and Destination Port
        sourcePort      = tcp.sport
        destinationPort = tcp.dport
```

The rest of the script uses the previously created classes:

```
class IPObservationDictionary:
class OSObservationDictionary:
```

.. along with the same packet processing code that was developed during the
P2NMAP-Capture.py script. The full script is included here:

P2NMAP-PCAP-Extractor.py Script

```
'''
Copyright (c) 2015 Chet Hosmer, cdh@python-forensics.org

Permission is hereby granted, free of charge, to any person obtaining a copy of this software
and associated documentation files (the "Software"), to deal in the Software without restriction,
including without limitation the rights to use, copy, modify, merge, publish, distribute,
sublicense, and/or sell copies of the Software, and permit persons to whom the Software is
furnished to do so, subject the following condition.
The above copyright notice and this permission notice shall be included in all copies or
substantial portions of the Software.

'''
#
# Process .pcap files
# Create   .ipdict and .osDict result files
#          suitable for analysis with P2NMAP-Analyze
#                              and  P2NMAP-OS-Fingerprint

# import support functions

import argparse                # Python Standard Library Parsing Module
import os                      # Python Standard Library OS module
import sys                     # Python Standard Library SYS Module
import socket                  # Python Standard Library socket module
import time                    # Python Standard Library time module
import datetime                # Python Standard Library datetime module
import pickle                  # Python Standard Library pickling module

import dpkt                    # 3rd Party Packet Parsing Module
                               # pip install dptk    to intall the module
from dpkt.udp import UDP       # Import specific objects from DPKT for convience
from dpkt.tcp import TCP       #

# CONSTANTS

HOUR_INDEX = 3                 # Index of the Hour value in the Time Structure

#
# Name: ValDirWrite
#
# Desc: Function that will validate a directory path as
#       existing and writable.  Used for argument validation only
#
# Input: a directory path string
#
# Actions:
#              if valid will return the Directory String
#
#              if invalid it will raise an ArgumentTypeError within argparse
#              which will inturn be reported by argparse to the user
#

def ValDirWrite(theDir):

    # Validate the path is a directory
    if not os.path.isdir(theDir):
        raise argparse.ArgumentTypeError('Directory does not exist')
```

```
    # Validate the path is writable
    if os.access(theDir, os.W_OK):
        return theDir
    else:
        raise argparse.ArgumentTypeError('Directory is not writable')

#End ValDirWrite ======================================


#
# Name: ValidateFileRead Function
#
# Desc: Function that will validate that a file exists and is readable
#
# Input: A file name with full path
#
# Actions:
#               if valid will return path
#
#               if invalid it will raise an ArgumentTypeError within argparse
#               which will inturn be reported by argparse to the user
#

def ValFileRead(theFile):

    # Validate the path is a valid
    if not os.path.exists(theFile):
        raise argparse.ArgumentTypeError('File does not exist')

    # Validate the path is readable
    if os.access(theFile, os.R_OK):
        return theFile
    else:
        raise argparse.ArgumentTypeError('File is not readable')

#End ValidateFileRead ======================================


#
# Class: IPObservationDictionary
#
# Desc: Handles all methods and properties
#       relating to the IPOservations
#
#

class IPObservationDictionary:

    # Constructor

    def __init__(self):

        #Attributes of the Object

        self.Dictionary = {}             # Dictionary to Hold IP Observations

    # Method to Add an observation

    def AddOb(self, key, hour):

        # Check to see if key is already in the dictionary
```

```
        if key in self.Dictionary:

            # If yes, retrieve the current value
            curValue = self.Dictionary[key]

            # Increment the count for the current hour
            curValue[hour-1] = curValue[hour-1] + 1

            # Update the value associated with this key
            self.Dictionary[key] = curValue

        else:
            # if the key doesn't yet exist
            # Create one

            curValue = [0,0,0,0,0,0,0,0,0,0,0,0,0,0,0,0,0,0,0,0,0,0,0,0]

            # Increment the count for the current hour
            curValue[hour-1] = curValue[hour-1] + 1

            self.Dictionary[key] = curValue

# Print the Contents of the Dictionary

def PrintOb(self):
    print "\nIP Observations"
    print "Unique Combinations:     ", str(len(self.Dictionary))
    print

    # Print Heading

    print '                                               ',
    print "|--------------------------------------- Hourly Observations  ---------------
-------------------------------|"
    print '%16s' % "Server",
    print '%16s' % "Client",
    print '%7s'  % "Port",
    print '%5s'  % "Type",

    for i in range(0, 24):
        print ' ',
        print '%02d' % i,
    print

    sorted = self.Dictionary.items()
    sorted.sort()

    # Print Contents
    for keys,values in sorted:

        print '%16s' % keys[0],
        print '%16s' % keys[1],
        print '%7s'  % str(keys[2]),
        print '%5s'  % keys[3],

        for i in range(0, 24):
            print '%4s' % str(values[i]),
        print

# Save the Current Observation Dictionary
# to the specified file
```

```python
    def SaveOb(self, fileName):

        with open(fileName, 'wb') as fp:
            pickle.dump(self.Dictionary, fp)

    # Destructor Delete the Object

    def __del__(self):
        if VERBOSE:
            print "Closed"

# End IPObservationClass ======================================

#
# Class: OSObservationDictionary
#
# Desc: Handles all methods and properties
#       relating to the OSObservations
#
#

class OSObservationDictionary:

    # Constructor

    def __init__(self):

        #Attributes of the Object

        self.Dictionary = {}                # Dictionary to Hold IP Observations

    # Method to Add an observation

    def AddOb(self, key, hour):

        # Check to see if key is already in the dictionary

        if key in self.Dictionary:

            # If yes, retrieve the current value
            curValue = self.Dictionary[key]
            # Increment the count for the current hour
            curValue[hour-1] = curValue[hour-1] + 1

            # Update the value associated with this key
            self.Dictionary[key] = curValue

        else:
            # if the key doesn't yet exist
            # Create one

            curValue = [0,0,0,0,0,0,0,0,0,0,0,0,0,0,0,0,0,0,0,0,0,0,0,0]

            # Increment the count for the current hour
            curValue[hour-1] = curValue[hour-1] + 1

            self.Dictionary[key] = curValue

    # Method to retrieve an observation
    # If no observation found return None

    def GetOb(self,key):
```

```python
            if key in self.Dictionary:
                curValue = self.Dictionary[key]
                return curValue
            else:
                return None

    # Print the Contents of the Dictionary

    def PrintOb(self):

        print "\nOS Observations"
        print "Unique Combinations:     ", str(len(self.Dictionary))
        print


        # Print Heading
        print '                                                 ',
        print "|----------------------------------------  Hourly Observations  ---------------
-----------------------------------|"

        print '%16s' % "Server",
        print '%4s'  % "TOS",
        print '%4s'  % "TTL",
        print '%6s'  % "DF",
        print '%7s'  % "Window",

        for i in range(0, 24):
            print ' ',
            print '%02d' % i,
        print "\n---------------------------------------------------------------------------
-------------------------------------------------------------------------"

        sorted = self.Dictionary.items()
        sorted.sort()

        # Print Contents
        for keys,values in sorted:
            print '%16s' % keys[0],
            print '%4s'  % str(keys[1]),
            print '%4s'  % str(keys[2]),
            print '%6s'  % str(keys[3]),
            print '%7s'  % str(keys[4]),

            for i in range(0, 24):
                print '%4s' % str(values[i]),
            print

    # End Print OS Observations
    # Save the Current Observation Dictionary
    # to the specified file

    def SaveOb(self, fileName):

        with open(fileName, 'wb') as fp:
            pickle.dump(self.Dictionary, fp)

    # Destructor Delete the Object
```

```
        def __del__(self):
            if VERBOSE:
                print "Closed"

# End OSObservationClass =====================================

#======================================
#
# Main Program Starts Here
#======================================

if __name__ == '__main__':

    # Setup Argument Parser Object

    parser = argparse.ArgumentParser('P2NAMP PCAP Extractor')

    parser.add_argument('-v', '--verbose', help="Provide Progress Messages", action='store_true')
    parser.add_argument('-o', '--outPath', type= ValDirWrite, required=True, help="Output
Directory")
    parser.add_argument('-i', '--inFile' , type= ValFileRead, required=True, help="PCAP input
File - Full Path")

    #process the command arguments

    cmdArgs = parser.parse_args()

    # convert arguments to simple local variables

    VERBOSE    = cmdArgs.verbose
    inFile     = cmdArgs.inFile
    outPath    = cmdArgs.outPath

    if VERBOSE:
        print "Packet Parsing Algorithm, version 1.0"
        print

        print "Opening Capture File: "+ inFile
        print


    # Create IP observation dictionary object
    ipOB = IPObservationDictionary()
    osOB = OSObservationDictionary()

    # Loop through all the packets found in the pcap file
    # Obtain the timestamp and packet data

    if VERBOSE:
        print "Processing PCAP, please wait ...\n"

    # Use dpkt and setup a pcapReader Object
    try:
        # Create pcapReader Object
        pcapReader = dpkt.pcap.Reader(file(inFile, "rb"))
    except:
        # Error Reading pcap
        print "Error importing: ", infile
        quit()
    # Using the pcapReader Object process the
    # the contents of the selected pcap file
```

```
# each interation through the loop will return
# 1) packet timestamp
# 2) packet raw data

for timeStamp, pckData in pcapReader:

    # Next I retrieve the etherNet packet contents
    # and verify that it is an ethernet packet

    etherNet = dpkt.ethernet.Ethernet(pckData)

    # Verify that this ethernet packet carries an IP Packet

    if etherNet.type == dpkt.ethernet.ETH_TYPE_IP:

        # get the ip data and extract the source and destination ip addresses
        # use the socket module to convert them to dot notational form

        # Decode the source and destination IP Address
        ip = etherNet.data
        sourceAddress      = socket.inet_ntoa(ip.src)
        destinationAddress = socket.inet_ntoa(ip.dst)

        # Check Packet Type (either TCP or UDP and process accordingly)

        if type(ip.data) == TCP :

            # Extract and Decode the Ports in use
            tcp = ip.data

            # Obtain Data for OS Fingerprinting

            # SYN Flag
            SYN = ( tcp.flags & dpkt.tcp.TH_SYN ) != 0

            # DF Flag
            DF = ( tcp.flags & dpkt.tcp.TH_URG ) != 0

            # Window Size
            WINDOW_SIZE = tcp.win

            # Time to Live and Type of Service values
            TTL = ip.ttl
            TOS = ip.tos

            # Now obtain the Source and Destination Port
            sourcePort      = tcp.sport
            destinationPort = tcp.dport

            if sourcePort <= 1024:              # Assume server IP is server
                serverIP   = sourceAddress
                clientIP   = destinationAddress
                serverPort = sourcePort
                status = True
            elif destinationPort <= 1024:       # Assume destination IP is server
                serverIP   = destinationAddress
                clientIP   = sourceAddress
                serverPort = destinationPort
                status = True
            elif sourcePort <= destinationPort: # Assume server IP is server
                serverIP   = sourceAddress
                clientIP   = destinationAddress
```

```
            serverPort = sourcePort
            status = True
        elif sourcePort > destinationPort:   # Assume distinatin IP is server
            serverIP   = destinationAddress
            clientIP   = sourceAddress
            serverPort = destinationPort
            status = True
        else:                                # Should never get here
            serverIP   = "FILTER"
            clientIP   = "FILTER"
            serverPort = "FILTER"
            status = False

        # Convert the timestamp (epoch value)
        # into a time structure
        timeStruct = time.gmtime(timeStamp)

        # extract the hour the packet was captured
        theHour = timeStruct[HOUR_INDEX]

        if status:
            # Add a new IP observation and the hour
            ipOB.AddOb((serverIP, clientIP, serverPort, "TCP"), theHour)

            # If SYN is set also add a new OS Observation
            if SYN:
                osOB.AddOb( (serverIP, TOS, TTL, DF, WINDOW_SIZE), theHour)


elif type(ip.data) == UDP :

    # Extract and Decode the Ports in use
    udp = ip.data
    sourcePort      = udp.sport
    destinationPort = udp.dport

    if sourcePort <= 1024:              # Assume server IP is server
        serverIP   = sourceAddress
        clientIP   = destinationAddress
        serverPort = sourcePort
        status = True
    elif destinationPort <= 1024:      # Assume destination IP is server
        serverIP   = destinationAddress
        clientIP   = sourceAddress
        serverPort = destinationPort
        status = True
    elif sourcePort <= destinationPort: # Assume server IP is server
        serverIP   = sourceAddress
        clientIP   = destinationAddress
        serverPort = sourcePort
        status = True
    elif sourcePort > destinationPort:  # Assume distinatin IP is server
        serverIP   = destinationAddress
        clientIP   = sourceAddress
        serverPort = destinationPort
        status = True
    else:                               # Should never get here
        serverIP   = "FILTER"
        clientIP   = "FILTER"
        serverPort = "FILTER"
        status = False
```

```
                        # Convert the timestamp (epoch value)
                        # into a time structure

                        timeStruct = time.gmtime(timeStamp)
                        theHour = timeStruct[3]

                        if status:
                            # Add a new observation and the hour
                            ipOB.AddOb((serverIP, clientIP, serverPort, "UDP"), theHour)
                    else:
                        # Skip the Packet NOT TCP or UDP
                        continue
            else:
                # skip this packet NOT Ethernet Type
                continue

    # Once all packets are processed
    # Print out Results

    if VERBOSE:

        ipOB.PrintOb()
        osOB.PrintOb()

        print "\nSaving Observations ext: .ipDict and .osDict"

    # Save observations in our compatible format

    ipOutFile = datetime.datetime.now().strftime("%Y%m%d-%H%M%S")+".ipDict"
    ipOutput  = os.path.join(outPath, ipOutFile)

    osOutFile = datetime.datetime.now().strftime("%Y%m%d-%H%M%S")+".osDict"
    osOutput  = os.path.join(outPath, osOutFile)

    ipOB.SaveOb(ipOutput)
    osOB.SaveOb(osOutput)

    print 'Processing Complete'
```

Executing P2NMAP-PCAP-Extractor

Executing the PCAP-Extractor is done from the command line (again, Windows command shell along with Linux / Mac Shells all operate the same).

```
C:\CH5>python P2NMAP-PCAP-Extractor.py -h


usage: P2NAMP PCAP Extractor [-h] [-v] -o OUTPATH -i INFILE

optional arguments:
  -h, --help            show this help message and exit
  -v, --verbose         Provide Progress Messages
  -o OUTPATH, --outPath OUTPATH
                        Output Directory
  -i INFILE, --inFile INFILE
                        PCAP input File - Full Path
```

```
C:\CH5>python P2NMAP-PCAP-Extractor.py -v -i ./PCAP/test.pcap -o ./OUT/

Packet Parsing Algorithm, version 1.0

Opening Capture File: ./PCAP/test.pcap

Processing PCAP, please wait ...
```

Executing the script with the –h option only, provides the argument list. Only 3 arguments are available:

- -v (optional) which will provide a verbose output from the application
- –i which is the input file and specifies the pcap file to extract from
- –o which specifies the output directory where the resulting .ipDict and. osDict files will be written with the familiar timestamp filename

When the script is executed with the verbose argument the following sample output is also generated on screen. (note: this output has been abridged to save space).

```
Packet Parsing Algorithm, version 1.0

Opening Capture File: ./PCAP/test.pcap

Processing PCAP, please wait ...


IP Observations
Unique Combinations:     3984
```

Server	Client	Port	Type	00	01	02	03	04	05	06	07	08	09	10	11	12	13	14	15	16	17	18	19	20	21	22	23
0.0.0.0	255.255.255.255	68	UDP	0	0	0	0	0	0	0	0	0	0	0	0	0	0	0	0	0	0	0	0	0	3	0	0
107.20.103.220	172.16.133.26	443	TCP	0	0	0	0	0	0	0	0	0	0	0	0	0	0	0	0	0	0	0	0	0	663	0	0
107.20.158.52	172.16.133.153	8080	TCP	0	0	0	0	0	0	0	0	0	0	0	0	0	0	0	0	0	0	0	0	0	708	0	0
107.20.161.243	172.16.133.48	443	TCP	0	0	0	0	0	0	0	0	0	0	0	0	0	0	0	0	0	0	0	0	0	57	0	0
107.20.170.67	172.16.133.63	443	TCP	0	0	0	0	0	0	0	0	0	0	0	0	0	0	0	0	0	0	0	0	0	40	0	0
107.20.203.158	172.16.133.121	80	TCP	0	0	0	0	0	0	0	0	0	0	0	0	0	0	0	0	0	0	0	0	0	20	0	0
107.20.206.100	172.16.133.54	80	TCP	0	0	0	0	0	0	0	0	0	0	0	0	0	0	0	0	0	0	0	0	0	36	0	0
107.20.217.22	172.16.133.93	80	TCP	0	0	0	0	0	0	0	0	0	0	0	0	0	0	0	0	0	0	0	0	0	6	0	0
107.20.231.134	172.16.133.16	80	TCP	0	0	0	0	0	0	0	0	0	0	0	0	0	0	0	0	0	0	0	0	0	9	0	0
107.20.232.172	172.16.133.132	80	TCP	0	0	0	0	0	0	0	0	0	0	0	0	0	0	0	0	0	0	0	0	0	24	0	0

Hourly Observations

```
...
...  Output Abridged
...

OS Observations
Unique Combinations:      2477

                                                  |------------------------------------------ Hourly
Observations   ------------------------------------------------|
            Server  TOS  TTL     DF  Window   00    01    02    03    04    05    06    07    08    09    10
11    12    13    14    15    16    17    18    19    20    21    22    23
------------------------------------------------------------------------------------------------------
------------------------------------------------------------------------------
    107.20.103.220    0  128  False    8192    0     0     0     0     0     0     0     0     0     0     0
0     0     0     0     0     0     0     0     0     0     2     0     0
    107.20.103.220   32   44  False    5840    0     0     0     0     0     0     0     0     0     0     0
0     0     0     0     0     0     0     0     0     0     2     0     0
    107.20.161.243    0  128  False    8192    0     0     0     0     0     0     0     0     0     0     0
0     0     0     0     0     0     0     0     0     0     3     0     0
    107.20.161.243   32   42  False    5840    0     0     0     0     0     0     0     0     0     0     0
0     0     0     0     0     0     0     0     0     0     3     0     0
    107.20.170.67     0  128  False    8192    0     0     0     0     0     0     0     0     0     0     0
0     0     0     0     0     0     0     0     0     0     2     0     0
    107.20.170.67    32   42  False   14600    0     0     0     0     0     0     0     0     0     0     0
0     0     0     0     0     0     0     0     0     0     2     0     0

Saving Observations ext: .ipDict and .osDict
Processing Complete
```

Now you can utilize the resulting files from this run:

> 20150303-151016.ipDict
> 20150303-151016.osDict

Now that we have generated the extracted ipDict and osDict files we can utilize P2NMAP-Analyze.py or P2NMAP-OS-Fingerprint.py to perform the requisite analysis. Note the P2NMAP-OS.Fingerpring.py script will be discussed in the next section.

Where do you find .pcap files to experiment with? You can obviously perform a Google search and you will find quite a few potential sources. However, three sources that I used heavily during experimentation include:

WireShark Samples Captures: http://wiki.wireshark.org/SampleCaptures

Tcpreplay: http://tcpreplay.appneta.com/wiki/captures.html

NETRESEC: http://www.netresec.com/?page=PcapFiles

Shown in Figure 5-1, Figure 5-2 and Figure 5-3

FIGURE 5-1 Wireshark Samples Captures Web Page.

FIGURE 5-2 Tcpreplay Sample Captures.

Experts in network security monitoring and network forensics

NETRESEC | Products | Resources | Blog | About Netresec |

NETRESEC > Resources > PCAP Files

Publicly available PCAP files

This is a list of public packet capture repositories, which are freely available on the internet. Most of the sites listed below share Full Packet Capture (FPC) files, but some do unfortunately only have truncated frames.

Computer Defence Exercises (CDX)

This category includes network traffic from exercises and competitions, such as Cyber Defense Exercises (CDX) and red-team/blue-team competitions.

MACCDC – Pcaps from National CyberWatch Mid–Atlantic Collegiate Cyber Defense Competition
http://www.netresec.com/?page=MACCDC

Captures from the "2009 Inter–Service Academy Cyber Defense Competition" served by Information Technology Operations Center (ITOC), United States Military Academy
https://www.itoc.usma.edu/research/dataset/

Capture the Flag Competitions (CTF)

PCAP files from capture-the-flag (CTF) competitions and challenges.

DEFCON Capture the Flag Contest traces (from DEF CON 8, 10 and 11)
http://cctf.shmoo.com/

DEFCON 17 Capture the Flag Contest traces

FIGURE 5-3 NETRESEC Sample Captures.

PASSIVE OS FINGERPRINTING

As many people are painfully aware, performing passive OS fingerprinting is a significant challenge. However, in this section I will provide the building blocks for identifying at least the general OS that is executing on the associated server platforms. The actual missing-link is a comprehensive dataset of rules that would more accurately map OS behaviors. This method is not meant to compete with the active methods of fingerprinting generated from the NMAP community, SAINT developers, McAfee/Intel Foundstone labs and other mainstream vendors. Rather the solution is presented to encourage expansion of the method, especially the painstaking task of developing signatures that will work during passive based examinations.

OS Fingerprinting Truth Table

During the passive collection of packet data (whether using P2NMAP-Capture. py or extracting packet data using P2NMAP-PCAP-Extractor.py) several key initial parameters were collected from observed packets. These IP packet values include Type of Service, Time to Live, Don't Fragment (DF) and Window Size. These values were only collected when the IP packet contained a TCP segment with the SYN flag set. This set of values allows for the creation of a Truth Table that would generate possible OS Fingerprinting when all four of the table values match the observed values.

> Truth Tables provide a method of defining all possible values that can exist for a certain set of facts, variables or functions. These tables contains multiple rows and columns, with the top row representing the category values along with a final column that contains the conclusion based on the values specified in that row.

Table 5-1 shows a sample table with a few sample entries.

In order to improve on the basic concept, I wanted a bit more flexibility in the table. First, the **Time to Live** observations are impacted by the number of router hops that the packets take between the source and destination. Thus even if the packet starts out at 128, the value we observe is likely to be less than 128, therefore I will make this a range of values instead of a fixed number. Secondly, for certain known fingerprint signatures only 2 of the values may be required for an accurate identification.

For example, we may have knowledge that a certain CISCO network device has a starting TTL value of 255 and a **Window Size** of 4128, but the **Type of Service** and **DF** flags are not relevant, unknown or unreliable. In this case I would like to ignore the **DF** and **TOS** fields during the comparison (by using wild cards). Finally, for ease of parsing the table, the **TTL** and **Window Size** fields will always contain a range. The resulting truth table would then look like that in Table 5-2.

Table 5-1 Basic Truth Table

Time to Live	Type of Service	DF Flag	Window Size	OS Identified
128	0	Y	5000-9000	Window NT
64	16	N	17520	Open BSD
128	0	Y	32000-32768	Netware

Table 5-2 Improved Truth Table

Time to Live	Type of Service	DF Flag	Window Size	OS Identified
65-128	0	Y	5000-9000	Window NT
33-64	16	N	17520-17520	Open BSD
65-128	0	Y	32000-32768	Netware
129-255	*	*	4128-4128	Cisco IOS

A sample flat file truth table file is shown here, with the syntax being strict space delimited columns to make parsing the file simple. The file can be expanded to contain additional values as more known observations become available or the fingerprint data improves.

```
17-32      0    N 8192-8192      Windows
65-128     0    Y 5000-9000      Windows
65-128     0    Y 17000-18000    Windows
65-129     0    Y 32000-32768    Netware
33-64      16   N 17520-17520    OpenBSD
33-64      0    N 5804-5840      HP
33-64      0    N 24820-24280    SCO
33-64      16   Y 17520-17520    FreeBSD
33-64      16   N 17520 17520    Linux
33-64      0    Y 24280-24280    Solaris
65-128     0    N 65535-65535    CISCO
33-60      0    Y 16000-16100    AIX43
33-60      0    N 16000-16100    AIX43
65-128     0    Y 5000-9000      Windwos
127-255    192  N 3800-5000      Cisco
33-64      *    * 5720-5840      Linux
33-64      *    * 65535-65535    BSD
65-128     *    * 8192-8192      Windows
129-255    *    * 4128-4128      CISCO
```

Truth Table Python Class

To handle the processing of the truth table, I create a simple class that will perform three basic functions:

1. Load the truth table and process the range values
2. Accept a known set (TTL, TOS, DF and Window Size) as input and return the first matching OS Fingerprint from the loaded truth table.
3. Print the truth table for convenience and verification

```python
class FingerPrint:

    # Constructor

    def __init__(self):

        self.classificationList = []

        self.osObservationsLoaded  = False
        self.osObservationFileName = ""
        self.osTruthTableLoaded = False
        self.osTruthTableFileName = ""
```

```
# Load in the TruthTable from the userdefined text file

def LoadTruthTable(self, truthTable):

    # String Index Values

    TTL_RANGE   = 0
    TOS         = 1
    DF          = 2
    WINDOW_SIZE = 3
    OS          = 4
    CHK_FLD     = 5
    tableErrors = False

    try:
        # Process the User Defined Input Table

        with open(truthTable, "r") as fileContents:

            for eachLine in fileContents:

                values = eachLine.split()

                # Make sure we have the proper number of fields
                # in this line

                if len(values) == CHK_FLD:
                    # convert the text ttl and winsize into low and high integers
                    # unless wild card specified
                    if values[TTL_RANGE] != '*':
                        ttlLow, ttlHigh = self.convertRange(values[TTL_RANGE])
                    else:
                        ttlLow = -1
                        ttlHgh = -1

                    if values[WINDOW_SIZE] != '*':
                        winLow, winHigh = self.convertRange(values[WINDOW_SIZE])
                    else:
                        winLow  = -1
                        winHigh = -1

                    #  Convert TOS to an integer, unless wild card
                    if values[TOS] == '*':
                        tosVal = '*'
                    else:
                        try:
                            tosVal = int(values[TOS])
                        except:
                            # invalid TOS value
                            # skip this line
                            tableErrors = True
                            continue

                    # Convert DF to True or False or wild card
                    if values[DF].upper()   == "Y":
                        dfVal = True
                    elif values[DF].upper() == "N":
                        dfVal = False
                    elif values[DF] == '*':
                        dfVal = "*"
```

```
                    else:
                        # invalid DF value
                        # skip this line
                        tableErrors = True
                        continue

                if ttlLow != None and winLow != None:
                    self.classificationList.append( [ttlLow, ttlHigh, tosVal, dfVal,
winLow, winHigh, values[OS]] )
                    else:
                        tableErrors = True

        self.osTruthTableLoaded   = True
        self.osTruthTableFileName = truthTable

    except:
        print "***** Loading Truth Table - Failed *****"
        self.osTruthTableLoaded = False
        self.osTruthTableFileName = ""

    # Return to caller with errors flag
    # True  = Errors Found in Text File
    # False = All Rows Loaded Properly
    return tableErrors

# End LoadTruthTable Method

# Convert Range Method
# Used to Convert range values 123-456
# into two integer values

def convertRange(self, theString):

    lowStr = ""
    hghStr = ""

    # parse the low value
    for x in range(0,len(theString)):
        if theString[x].isdigit():
            lowStr += theString[x]
        else:
            break
    # Skip the delimeters usually comma or dash
    for s in range(x, len(theString)):
        if theString[s].isdigit():
            break
        else:
            continue

    # If we are not at the end
    if s < len(theString):
        # parse the high value
        for y in range(s, len(theString)):
            if theString[y].isdigit():
                hghStr += theString[y]
            else:
                break
    else:
        return None, None

    # If we have two strings, then convert to ints
```

```
        if len(lowStr) > 0 and len(hghStr) > 0:
            lowVal = int(lowStr)
            hghVal = int(hghStr)
        else:
            return None, None

        # Finally,
        # If we have a proper low high relationship return the ints
        if lowVal <= hghVal:
            return lowVal, hghVal
        else:
            return None, None

    # End convertRange Method


    # GetOSClassification Searches the Loaded Truth Table
    # for a match, it will return on the first successful match
    # if no match is found it will return the string "UNDEFINED"

    def GetOSClassification(self, ttl, tos, df, winSize):

        # List Index

        TTL_LOW    = 0
        TTL_HGH    = 1
        TOS_VAL    = 2
        DF_VAL     = 3
        WIN_LOW    = 4
        WIN_HGH    = 5
        OS_VAL     = 6
        # Search the classificationList (TruthTable)

        for entry in self.classificationList:

            # First Check the TTL Value, if in Range continue
            if ( (entry[TTL_LOW] <= ttl and entry[TTL_HGH] >= ttl) or (entry[TTL_LOW] == '*') ):
                # Next Check the Type of Service Value, if Match Continue
                if entry[TOS_VAL] == tos  or entry[TOS_VAL] == "*":
                    # Next Check the DF Flag, if Match Continue
                    if entry[DF_VAL] == df or entry[DF_VAL] == "*":
                        # Finally, check the Window Size, if in Range Continue
                        if ( (entry[WIN_LOW] <= winSize and entry[WIN_HGH] >= winSize) or
(entry[WIN_LOW] == '*') ):
                            # Return the OS Value Found
                            return entry[OS_VAL]

        # If none of the rules result in a match
        return "UNDEFINED"

    # End GetOSClassification Method


    # PrintTruthTable Method
    # Print out the currently loaded Truth Table
```

```
def PrintTruthTable(self):

    TTL_LOW     = 0
    TTL_HGH     = 1
    TOS_VAL     = 2
    DF_VAL      = 3
    WIN_LOW     = 4
    WIN_HGH     = 5
    OS_VAL      = 6

    print >> OUT,'\nCurrent Loaded Fingerprint Truth Table\n'
    print >> OUT,'%10s ' % 'TTL RANGE',

    print >> OUT,'%4s ' % 'TOS',
    print >> OUT,'%5s ' % ' DF ',

    print >> OUT,'%16s ' % 'WIN RANGE',

    print >> OUT,'%22s ' % 'OS Fingerprint'
    print >> OUT,'================================================================='

    for entry in self.classificationList:

        print >> OUT,'%3s ' % str(entry[TTL_LOW]),
        print >> OUT, "-",
        print >> OUT,'%3s ' % str(entry[TTL_HGH]),

        print >> OUT,'%4s ' % str(entry[TOS_VAL]),
        print >> OUT,'%5s ' % str(entry[DF_VAL]),

        print >> OUT,'%6s ' % str(entry[WIN_LOW]),
        print >> OUT, "-",
        print >> OUT,'%6s ' % str(entry[WIN_HGH]),

        print >> OUT,' %20s '% entry[OS_VAL]

    print >> OUT, '\n\n'

# End PrintTruthTable Method
```

Now that we can load and process the truth table, all that is left to do is build a menu driven script that can:

1. Load a previously generated .osDict file
2. Load and process and user defined truth table
3. Generate the OS fingerprint results

In addition, I have provided similar support functions as with the P2NMAP-Analyze script to allow directing the output to a file, along with the ability to print the contents of the .osDict observations and the truth table contents.

P2NMAP-OS-Fingerprint Script

```
' ' '
Copyright (c) 2015 Chet Hosmer, cdh@python-forensics.org

Permission is hereby granted, free of charge, to any person obtaining a copy of this software
and associated documentation files (the "Software"), to deal in the Software without restriction,
including without limitation the rights to use, copy, modify, merge, publish, distribute,
sublicense, and/or sell copies of the Software, and permit persons to whom the Software is
furnished to do so, subject the following condition.
The above copyright notice and this permission notice shall be included in all copies or
substantial portions of the Software.

' ' '


#
# P2NMA-Analyze.py Script
#
# Perform analysis of previously capture .ipdict files
#
#
# Version 1.0 February 17-2015

import argparse          # Python Standard Library - Parser for command-line options, arguments
import os                # operating system functions i.e. file I/o
import datetime          # Python Standard Library date and time methods
import pickle            # Python Standard Library pickle methods
import socket            # Python Standard Library Low Level Networking
import sys               # Python Standard Library Low Level System Methods

# PSUEDO CONSTANTS

PRINT_STDOUT    = True   # If True, all output and menu selections directed
                         # If False, all output directed to a file except menu

OUT             = sys.stdout       # Default Output to Standard Out
#
# Class: OSObservationDictionary
#
# Desc: Handles all methods and properties
#       relating to the OSObservations
#
#

class OSObservationDictionary:

    # Constructor

    def __init__(self):

        #Attributes of the Object

        self.Dictionary = {}              # Dictionary to Hold IP Observations
        self.osObservationFileName = ""
        self.osObservationsLoaded  = False
```

```
def LoadOb(self, fileName):
    try:
        with open(fileName, 'rb') as fp:
            self.Dictionary = pickle.loads(fp.read())
            self.observationFileName = fileName
            self.observationsLoaded  = True
    except:
        print "Loading OS Observations File - Failed"
        self.osObservationsLoaded  = False
        self.osObservationFileName = ""

    # Method to retrieve an observation
# If no observation found return None

def GetOb(self,key):

    if key in self.Dictionary:
        curValue = self.Dictionary[key]
        return curValue
    else:
        return None

def GetAllObservations(self):

    observationList = []

    sorted = self.Dictionary.items()
    sorted.sort()

    for k, v in sorted:
        observationList.append(k)

    return observationList

def PrintOb(self):

    print >> OUT, "\nOS Observations"
    print >> OUT, "Unique Combinations:    ", str(len(self.Dictionary))
    print >> OUT


    # Print Heading
    print >> OUT, '                                                     ',
    print >> OUT, "|----------------------------------------- Hourly Observations  -------
-------------------------------------------|"

    print >> OUT, '%16s' % "Server",
    print >> OUT, '%4s'  % "TOS",
    print >> OUT, '%4s'  % "TTL",
    print >> OUT, '%6s'  % "DF",
    print >> OUT, '%7s'  % "Window",

    for i in range(0, 24):
        print >> OUT,  ' ',
        print >> OUT, '%02d' % i,
    print >> OUT, "\n------------------------------------------------------------------------
--------------------------------------------------------------------"

    sorted = self.Dictionary.items()
    sorted.sort()
```

```python
        # Print Contents
        for keys,values in sorted:
            print >> OUT, '%16s' % keys[0],
            print >> OUT, '%4s'  % str(keys[1]),
            print >> OUT, '%4s'  % str(keys[2]),
            print >> OUT, '%6s'  % str(keys[3]),
            print >> OUT, '%7s'  % str(keys[4]),

            for i in range(0, 24):
                print >> OUT, '%4s' % str(values[i]),
            print >> OUT

    # End Print OS Observations

    # Load in and Observation Dictionary
    # from the specified file

    def LoadOb(self, fileName):

        try:
            with open(fileName, 'rb') as fp:
                self.Dictionary = pickle.loads(fp.read())
                self.osObservationFileName = fileName
                self.osObservationsLoaded  = True
        except:
            print "Loading Observations - Failed"
            self.osObservationsLoaded  = False
            self.osObservationFileName = ""


    # Destructor Delete the Object

    def __del__(self):
        print >> OUT, "OS Observation Dictionary Closed"

# End OSObservationClass ======================================

class FingerPrint:

    # Constructor

    def __init__(self):

        self.classificationList = []

        self.osObservationsLoaded  = False
        self.osObservationFileName = ""
        self.osTruthTableLoaded = False
        self.osTruthTableFileName = ""

    # Load in the TruthTable from the userdefined text file

    def LoadTruthTable(self, truthTable):

        # String Index Values

        TTL_RANGE   = 0
        TOS         = 1
        DF          = 2
        WINDOW_SIZE = 3
```

```
OS          = 4
CHK_FLD     = 5

tableErrors = False

try:
    # Process the User Defined Input Table

    with open(truthTable, "r") as fileContents:

        for eachLine in fileContents:

            values = eachLine.split()

            # Make sure we have the proper number of fields
            # in this line

            if len(values) == CHK_FLD:
                # convert the text ttl and winsize into low and high integers
                # unless wild card specified
                if values[TTL_RANGE] != '*':
                    ttlLow, ttlHigh = self.convertRange(values[TTL_RANGE])
                else:
                    ttlLow = -1
                    ttlHgh = -1

                if values[WINDOW_SIZE] != '*':
                    winLow, winHigh = self.convertRange(values[WINDOW_SIZE])
                else:
                    winLow  = -1
                    winHigh = -1

                #  Convert TOS to an integer, unless wild card
                if values[TOS] == '*':
                    tosVal = '*'
                else:
                    try:
                        tosVal = int(values[TOS])
                    except:
                        # invalid TOS value
                        # skip this line
                        tableErrors = True
                        continue

                # Convert DF to True or False or wild card
                if values[DF].upper()   == "Y":
                    dfVal = True
                elif values[DF].upper() == "N":
                    dfVal = False
                elif values[DF] == '*':
                    dfVal = "*"
                else:
                    # invalid DF value
                    # skip this line
                    tableErrors = True
                    continue

                if ttlLow != None and winLow != None:
                    self.classificationList.append( [ttlLow, ttlHigh, tosVal, dfVal,
winLow, winHigh, values[OS]] )
                else:
                    tableErrors = True
```

```
            self.osTruthTableLoaded   = True
            self.osTruthTableFileName = truthTable

        except:
            print "***** Loading Truth Table - Failed *****"
            self.osTruthTableLoaded = False
            self.osTruthTableFileName = ""

        # Return to caller with errors flag
        # True  = Errors Found in Text File
        # False = All Rows Loaded Properly

        return tableErrors

# End LoadTruthTable Method

# Convert Range Method
# Used to Convert range values 123-456
# into two integer values

def convertRange(self, theString):

    lowStr = ""
    hghStr = ""

    # parse the low value
    for x in range(0,len(theString)):
        if theString[x].isdigit():
            lowStr += theString[x]
        else:
            break
    # Skip the delimeters usually comma or dash
    for s in range(x, len(theString)):
        if theString[s].isdigit():
            break
        else:
            continue

    # If we are not at the end
    if s < len(theString):
        # parse the high value
        for y in range(s, len(theString)):
            if theString[y].isdigit():
                hghStr += theString[y]
            else:
                break
    else:
        return None, None

    # If we have two strings, then convert to ints

    if len(lowStr) > 0 and len(hghStr) > 0:
        lowVal = int(lowStr)
        hghVal = int(hghStr)
    else:
        return None, None

    # Finally,
    # If we have a proper low high relationship return the ints
    if lowVal <= hghVal:
        return lowVal, hghVal
    else:
        return None, None

# End convertRange Method
```

```python
    # GetOSClassification Searches the Loaded Truth Table
    # for a match, it will return on the first successful match
    # if no match is found it will return the string "UNDEFINED"

    def GetOSClassification(self, ttl, tos, df, winSize):

        # List Index

        TTL_LOW      = 0
        TTL_HGH      = 1
        TOS_VAL      = 2
        DF_VAL       = 3
        WIN_LOW      = 4
        WIN_HGH      = 5
        OS_VAL       = 6

        # Search the classificationList (TruthTable)

        for entry in self.classificationList:

            # First Check the TTL Value, if in Range continue
            if ( (entry[TTL_LOW] <= ttl and entry[TTL_HGH] >= ttl) or (entry[TTL_LOW] == '*') ):
                # Next Check the Type of Service Value, if Match Continue
                if entry[TOS_VAL] == tos  or entry[TOS_VAL] == "*":
                    # Next Check the DF Flag, if Match Continue
                    if entry[DF_VAL] == df or entry[DF_VAL] == "*":
                        # Finally, check the Window Size, if in Range Continue
                        if ( (entry[WIN_LOW] <= winSize and entry[WIN_HGH] >= winSize) or
(entry[WIN_LOW] == '*') ):
                            # Return the OS Value Found
                            return entry[OS_VAL]

        # If none of the rules result in a match
        return "UNDEFINED"

    # End GetOSClassification Method


    # PrintTruthTable Method
    # Print out the currently loaded Truth Table

    def PrintTruthTable(self):

        TTL_LOW      = 0
        TTL_HGH      = 1
        TOS_VAL      = 2
        DF_VAL       = 3
        WIN_LOW      = 4
        WIN_HGH      = 5
        OS_VAL       = 6

        print >> OUT,'\nCurrent Loaded Fingerprint Truth Table\n'
        print >> OUT,'%10s ' % 'TTL RANGE',

        print >> OUT,'%4s ' % 'TOS',
        print >> OUT,'%5s ' % ' DF ',

        print >> OUT,'%16s ' % 'WIN RANGE',

        print >> OUT,'%22s ' % 'OS Fingerprint'
        print >> OUT,'========================================================================'
```

```python
        for entry in self.classificationList:

            print >> OUT,'%3s ' % str(entry[TTL_LOW]),
            print >> OUT, "-",
            print >> OUT,'%3s ' % str(entry[TTL_HGH]),

            print >> OUT,'%4s ' % str(entry[TOS_VAL]),
            print >> OUT,'%5s ' % str(entry[DF_VAL]),

            print >> OUT,'%6s ' % str(entry[WIN_LOW]),
            print >> OUT, "-",
            print >> OUT,'%6s ' % str(entry[WIN_HGH]),

            print >> OUT,' %20s '% entry[OS_VAL]

        print >> OUT, '\n\n'

    # End PrintTruthTable Method

    # Print the OS Fingerprint Analysis Menu

    def PrintOSAnalysisMenu(self, osState, osFile):

        print "\n========== P2NMAP OS Fingerprint Analyze Menu ==========\n"

        if osState:
            print "Current Observation File: ", osFile
        if self.osTruthTableLoaded:
            print "Current OS Truth Table:   ", self.osTruthTableFileName

        print

        print "[L]    Load Observation File for Analysis"
        print "[T]    Load Observation Truth Table"

        if osState and self.osTruthTableLoaded:

            if PRINT_STDOUT:
                print "[O]    Direct Output to File   (Current = Stdout)"
            else:
                print "[O]    Direct Output to Stdout (Current = results.txt)"

            print "================================================================"
            print "[1]    Print Truth Table"
            print "[2]    Print Observations"
            print "[3]    Print Probable OS Fingerprint "
            print
        print "[X]    Exit P2NMAP Fingerprint Analysis"
        print

# End FingerPrint Class =====================================



#=====================================
# Main Program Starts Here
#=====================================
```

```python
if __name__ == '__main__':

    # Local Psuedo Constants
    IP  = 0
    TOS = 1
    TTL = 2
    DF  = 3
    WIN = 4

    # Instantiate the FingerPrint and OSObservationDictionary Objects
    fpOB = FingerPrint()
    osOB = OSObservationDictionary()

    # Process User Input
    while True:
        fpOB.PrintOSAnalysisMenu(osOB.osObservationsLoaded, osOB.osObservationFileName)
        menuSelection = raw_input("Enter Selection: ").upper()

        # Attempt to Load the OS Capture File
        if menuSelection == 'L':
            fileName = raw_input("Enter OS Capture File: ")
            osOB.LoadOb(fileName)
            print

        # Attempt to Load a Truth Table
        elif menuSelection == 'T':
            fileName  = raw_input("Enter Truth Table File: ")
            rowErrors = fpOB.LoadTruthTable(fileName)

            # If Table Loaded, then check for row errors
            if fpOB.osTruthTableLoaded:
                # If rowError then inform the user
                if rowErrors:
                    print >> OUT, "Table Loaded but with Errors, Check Truth Table Input"
                else:
                    print >> OUT, "Truth Table Loaded"
                print

        # Toggle the Current Output State
        elif menuSelection == 'O':
            if PRINT_STDOUT:
                PRINT_STDOUT = False
                OUT = open("results.txt", 'w+')
            else:
                PRINT_STDOUT = True
                OUT.close()
                OUT = sys.stdout

        # Print Out the Current Truth Table

        elif menuSelection == '1':
            fpOB.PrintTruthTable()


        # Print out the Current Observation List
        elif menuSelection == '2':
            osOB.PrintOb()

        # Process the Observation List and
        # Print out Server Type
        # By matching the observed value list with
        # the loaded Truth Table
```

```
    elif menuSelection == '3':

        obList = osOB.GetAllObservations()

        print >> OUT
        print >> OUT,'%16s ' % 'IP Address',
        print >> OUT,'%25s ' % 'Fingerprint OS Type'
        print >> OUT,"=========================================================="

        for entry in obList:
            osType = fpOB.GetOSClassification(entry[TTL], entry[TOS], entry[DF], entry[WIN])
            print >> OUT,'%16s ' % entry[IP],
            print >> OUT,'%25s ' % osType


    elif menuSelection == 'X':
        break
    else:
        print "Entry not recognized"
        continue

    OUT.flush()

print "done"
```

Executing P2NMAP-OS-Fingerprint

Operating P2NMAP-OS-Fingerprint.py, requires no command line arguments
as the user is prompted for all necessary input.

```
C:\CH5>python P2NMAP-OS-FingerPrint.py

========== P2NMAP OS Fingerprint Analyze Menu ==========


[L]    Load Observation File for Analysis
[T]    Load Observation Truth Table
[X]    Exit P2NMAP Fingerprint Analysis

Enter Selection:
```

Before processing and generating the OS Fingerprints a valid observation file
and a valid truth table must be provided: Once this is accomplished successfully, the menu will change to allow for the execution of the remaining options:

1. Print truth table
2. Print observations
3. Print probable OS fingerprint

```
========== P2NMAP OS Fingerprint Analyze Menu ==========

Current Observation File:  test1.osDict
Current OS Truth Table:    fptt.txt

[L]    Load Observation File for Analysis
[T]    Load Observation Truth Table
[O]    Direct Output to File    (Current = Stdout)
================================================================
[1]    Print Truth Table
[2]    Print Observations
[3]    Print Probable OS Fingerprint

[X]    Exit P2NMAP Fingerprint Analysis

Enter Selection:  1
```

Selecting Option 1, produces the following truth table output, (Current Loaded Fingerprint Truth Table).

TTL RANGE	TOS	DF	WIN RANGE	OS Fingerprint
17 - 32	0	False	8192 - 8192	Windows
65 - 128	0	True	5000 - 9000	Windows
65 - 128	0	True	17000 - 18000	Windows
65 - 129	0	True	32000 - 32768	Netware
33 - 64	16	False	17520 - 17520	OpenBSD
33 - 64	0	False	5804 - 5840	HP
33 - 64	16	True	17520 - 17520	FreeBSD
33 - 64	0	True	24280 - 24280	Solaris
65 - 128	0	False	65535 - 65535	CISCO
33 - 60	0	True	16000 - 16100	AIX43
33 - 60	0	False	16000 - 16100	AIX43
65 - 128	0	True	5000 - 9000	Windwos
127 - 255	192	False	3800 - 5000	Cisco
33 - 64	*	*	5720 - 5840	Linux
33 - 64	*	*	65535 - 65535	BSD
65 - 128	*	*	8192 - 8192	Windows
129 - 255	*	*	4128 - 4128	CISCO

Selecting Option 2, produces the familiar (abridged) OS Observations result

```
========== P2NMAP OS Fingerprint Analyze Menu ==========

Current Observation File:  test1.osDict
Current OS Truth Table:    fptt.txt

[L]    Load Observation File for Analysis
[T]    Load Observation Truth Table
[O]    Direct Output to File   (Current = Stdout)
================================================================
[1]    Print Truth Table
[2]    Print Observations
[3]    Print Probable OS Fingerprint

[X]    Exit P2NMAP Fingerprint Analysis

Enter Selection: 2
```

```
OS Observations
Unique Combinations:    2477

                                              |---------------------------------------------  Hourly
Observations  --------------------------------------------------------|
             Server  TOS  TTL    DF  Window   00   01   02   03  04   05   06   07   08   09   10
11    12   13   14   15   16   17   18   19   20   21   22   23
----------------------------------------------------------------------------------------------
-------------------------------------------------------------------
   107.20.103.220    0  128  False    8192    0    0    0    0   0    0    0    0    0    0    0
0    0    0    0    0    0    0    0    0    0    2    0    0
   107.20.161.243    0  128  False    8192    0    0    0    0   0    0    0    0    0    0    0
0    0    0    0    0    0    0    0    0    0    3    0    0
   107.20.170.67     0  128  False    8192    0    0    0    0   0    0    0    0    0    0    0
0    0    0    0    0    0    0    0    0    0    2    0    0
   107.20.170.67    32   42  False   14600    0    0    0    0   0    0    0    0    0    0    0
0    0    0    0    0    0    0    0    0    0    2    0    0
```

Finally, Selecting Option 3, produces the (abridged) Probable OS Fingerprint Result

```
========== P2NMAP OS Fingerprint Analyze Menu ==========

Current Observation File:   test1.osDict
Current OS Truth Table:     fptt.txt

[L]     Load Observation File for Analysis
[T]     Load Observation Truth Table
[O]     Direct Output to File    (Current = Stdout)
=========================================================
[1]     Print Truth Table
[2]     Print Observations
[3]     Print Probable OS Fingerprint

[X]     Exit P2NMAP Fingerprint Analysis

Enter Selection:  3



        IP Address          Fingerprint OS Type
=========================================================
   107.20.103.220                   Linux
   107.20.161.243                   Linux
    107.20.170.67                   Windows
...

...

...


    98.139.51.132                   BSD
    98.142.99.171                   Linux
    99.61.13.155                    Windows
```

REVIEW

I tackled extracting key data from pcap files to convert them into the .ipDict and .osDict format in Chapter 5. This provides a direct way of handling captured network traffic from sources other than P2NMAP-Capture.py developed in Chapter 3. This was critical since more and more organizations are routinely collecting, preserving and retaining pcap files in their normal course of business. To extract the data, we used the 3rd Party Python Library dpkt, and were able to accomplish this core extraction process in less than 20 lines of code. I then wrapped this process into a script to automatically perform the functions.

Next, for the first time we used the contents of the .osDict file to make use of the observed TTL, TOS, DF and Window Size to predict the OS Type of the server in question. I defined a method using a truth table to perform this operation, and provided a baseline for further expansion of the truth table to improve the accuracy of the fingerprint identification. Next, I created the complete script, P2NMAP-OS-Fingerprint.py, to experiment with this new method of OS identification.

I also provided sample script execution for both P2NMAP-PCAP-Extractor and P2NMAP-OS-Fingerprint.

SUMMARY QUESTIONS

1. Challenge Problem 1: Develop experiments that generate observed behavior of a variety of operating systems under normal operation. Use that data to improve the truth table and ultimately the accuracy of Passive OS Fingerprint identification.
2. Challenge Problem 2: Utilize the ipDict result and the port values obtained to further improve OS Fingerprint identification by creating a truth table that provides association of known ports with the most operating system most probably in use.
3. Challenge Problem 3: Modify both P2NMAP-Capture.py and P2NMAP-PCAP-Extractor.py to collecting TTL, TOS, DF and Window Size observations for protocols other than TCP/UDP.

Additional Resources

Song Dug, dptk Python Package, https://pypi.python.org/pypi/dpkt

Silverman Jeffery, dptk documentation, http://www.commercialventvac.com/dpkt.html

## CHAPTER 6

Future Considerations and Challenge Problems

"There are two levers for moving men: interest and fear."

Napoleon Bonaparte

AUTHOR OBSERVATIONS

Developing this text and the associated scripts has been quite enjoyable. At the outset, my goal was to develop a text and scripts written in Python to perform the foundation of passive network mapping. This foundation has many uses and my hope is that it will continue to evolve.

In a world where we need to strike an achievable balance between security and privacy, I believe the concepts shared in this book provide the beginnings and underpinnings of that balance. None of the scripts or methods provided here analyze or expose the contents of network packets, rather they only focus on the end-to-end connections and key header information.

> According to 18 U.S. Code § 3121 "a government agency authorized to install and use a pen register or trap and trace device under this chapter or under State law shall use technology reasonably available to it that restricts the recording or decoding of electronic or other impulses to the dialing, routing, addressing, and signaling information utilized in the processing and transmitting of wire or electronic communications so as **not to include the contents** of any wire or electronic communications"

I wanted to make sure that the P2NMAP scripts met these requirements for two basic reasons:

1. I wanted the scripts to be usable in a wide range of lawful situations both by law enforcement and within corporate environments.
2. I wanted to demonstrate that staying within these limits could provide a useful and extensible toolset. The results of this first step may generate enough probable cause to generate a warrant that would then allow the examination of content.

Additionally, my goal was to create a full open source solution in order to:

1. Provide a baseline for other researchers, developers, academics and students, allowing them to advance the scripts to suit their specific needs.
2. Demonstrate that it was possible to create a Python-only source code solution for the capture, analysis and OS Fingerprinting of observed network traffic.
3. Provide a solution that could be safely deployed in environments where it could be dangerous to perform active network mapping, where damage to, or shutdown of critical information systems could occur, (e.g. SCADA environments).
4. Provide a Python-only solution where the resulting scripts would be portable across a wide range of computing platforms.
5. Finally, to allow the review by others to ensure that what has been presented meets these goals and objectives.

AUTHOR PREDICTIONS

FIGURE 6-1 Future Predictions.

Due to the combination of....

- strengthening security controls
- mobile device integration

- the broad acceptance of Bring Your Own Device (BYOD) models
- the entrée of wearable networked devices
- the movement toward the Internet of Things (IOT) philosophies
- the increased use of data leak prevention systems
- the improved application of firewalls, content filters
- the widespread deployment of intrusion prevention apparatus within corporate infrastructures
- and the continued reduction in the cost of data storage devices

…. the following predictions seem reasonable:

1. Monitoring (in other words, continuous passive network capture) will increase dramatically. As the devices we utilize each day become more transient players in the networks we control, our ability to actively scan or map these activities will become almost impossible.
2. Our ability to track devices and the humans attached to them is already quite elusive, and will continue to become more difficult as the explosive nature of these devices we carry or wear expands.
3. The line between broadband and land based networks will continue to blur. Even today our devices automatically switch seamlessly from one wireless network, to another, to broadband and back again even when we don't leave our homes!
4. Our ability to mine this data and make sense of it will become vital, if we wish to solve crimes, ferret out malicious insiders, stop the leakage of personal or corporate information and one day pre-empt nefarious acts instead of just reacting to them once they become the latest New York Times headline. We obviously must change our tactics.

The New York Times

TECHNOLOGY

8 Recent Cyberattacks Against Big Businesses

By KEVIN GRANVILLE FEB. 5, 2015

✉ Email

f Share

🐦 Tweet

📰 Save

Cyberattacks have become an ever-increasing threat. The F.B.I. now ranks cybercrime as one of its top law enforcement activities, and President Obama's recently proposed budget would sharply increase spending on cybersecurity, to $14 billion. Here are some of the major attacks on United States businesses in recent years.

FIGURE 6-2 New York Times Technology Headline 2-5-2015.

Of course privacy concerns continue to expand as the digital footprint that we leave with every click, post, tweet, music/video download, App purchase or now even every time we start our car or open our fridge expands. These actions become fodder for government monitoring, commercial gains and potential criminal activity.

CHALLENGE PROBLEMS

Several key challenge problems exist that are logical next steps. These can be approached by individuals, graduate and undergraduate students (with assistance) and by organizations wishing to participate in the evolution of the P2NMAP technologies.

Challenge 1: Passive OS Fingerprints – The development a complete truth table or other decision making model for a wide variety of operating signatures is essential. This requires both an initial effort to develop the current baseline (moving back in time) as well as methods to measure new versions.

Challenge 2: IPv6 – The challenge of evolving P2NMAP scripts to support IPv6 environments is two-fold. First, in order to perform the same level of capture and analysis that is currently supported for IPv4. Second, to examine/analyze and observe IPv6 headers to identify key data elements that would improve OS Fingerprinting.

Challenge 3: Wireless Passive Network Mapping – P2NMAP today will capture connections from WiFi devices as they flow in and out of current network switches. However, providing the ability to passively capture and analyze wireless connection in the air and mapping their temporal behaviors would be beneficial.

Challenge 4: IP Activity Mapping – The current capture and analysis capabilities of P2NMAP provide the fundamental data necessary to map behavior by specific IP addresses (clients or servers). However, sorting, filtering and visualizing this behavior would add significant value to investigators.

Challenge 5: Cross IP Link Analysis – It is likely that multiple P2NMAP captures or PCAP files collected from multiple network vantages points or even geographically separated networks is likely. The ability to combine, process and analyze a set of captures would provide a more global perspective for investigators.

Challenge 6: Python 3.3x – Porting P2NMAP-Capture, P2NMAP-Analyze, P2NMAP-OS-Fingerprint and P2NMAP-PCAP-Extractor should prove to be fairly straight-forward. This is the reason I minimized the use of 3rd party packages which is typically the most difficult aspect relating to the port.

Challenge 7: GUI vs Command Line – Finally, the current P2NMAP scripts are command line based in order to focus on core details of passive capture, analysis and OS fingerprinting. However, there are certainly benefits to wrapping the core scripts into a GUI for ease of use, configuration, management of captures, reporting and general visualization.

MORE INFORMATION

For additional information, the latest source code downloads, updated truth tables and other P2NMAP information:

Visit:

www.python-forensics.org/

To contact the author directly:

cdh@python-forensics.org

Subject Index

Printed in the United States
By Bookmasters